PROJECT BASED LEARNING FOR ALL

Many ISTE+ASCD members
received this book as a
member benefit upon
its initial release.

Learn more at **www.iste-
ascd.org/member-books**

Praise for *Project Based Learning for All*

"*Project Based Learning for All: A Leader's Guide* is an extraordinary gift to educational leaders and systems-change agents alike. With deep moral clarity and practical wisdom, Bob Lenz and Lisa Mireles provide more than a road map... they offer a soulful invitation to lead with purpose, equity, and hope. Grounded in decades of experience and enriched by real-world stories, this book reframes leadership as an act of transformation, vision, and love. Every page speaks to what's possible when we trust students and the adults who serve them—to lead learning that truly matters."

—**Carlos Moreno**, co-executive director of Big Picture Learning and author of *Finding Your Leadership Soul: What Our Students Can Teach Us About Love, Care, and Vulnerability*

"How do we tap into the curiosity of students so that they are motivated to learn on their own and engaged in using their higher-order thinking skills? This is a critical question for educators who believe in the power of education to transform lives, and it is a question addressed in this important new book. At a time when AI and other forms of technology threaten to make our students lazier and less skillful, project based learning (PBL) may very well be an antidote that can unleash the imaginations and problem-solving abilities of students. This book is an excellent guide for educators who seek to use PBL to transform teaching and learning."

—**Pedro A. Noguera**, PhD, dean of Rossier School of Education and author of *A Search for Common Ground: Conversations About the Toughest Questions in K–12 Education*

"With clarity and urgency, *Project Based Learning for All* illustrates how PBL can be both rigorous and impactful when the right conditions are in place. Lenz and Mireles go beyond classroom strategies to spotlight the leadership moves and structural shifts needed to make deeper learning accessible in every school, for every learner. It's a must-read for leaders committed to meaningful, systemic change."

—**Katie Martin**, co-founder and co-CEO of Learner-Centered Collaborative and author of *Evolving Education* and *Learner-Centered Innovation*

"*Project Based Learning for All* is exactly the road map deeper learning leaders have been waiting for. Lenz and Mireles speak with earned experience and clarity, offering not just strategies but a compelling vision for transforming schools to prepare our children for a globally connected, automated, and dynamic world. This book makes the work tangible—connecting leadership, equity, and high-quality PBL in ways that resonate with practitioners, engage communities, and, most importantly, empower students."

—**Jason E. Glass**, EdD, superintendent, Laguna Beach Unified School District, and former State Education Chief (KY & IA)

"As a former leader of a project based school, I was often asked, 'Who should we work with to make PBL equitable, practical, and scalable across schools, districts and communities?' My answer never changed: Talk to Bob Lenz and Lisa Mireles. *Project Based Learning for All* brings their expertise straight to you—blending stories, research, and elegant frameworks with reflection prompts and activities to help shape your own vision. It's the book I wish I'd had at the start: a trusted design guide to imagine boldly, lead with purpose, and create deeper learning experiences for each and every student. This is your design guide to the future."

—**Laura McBain**, managing director of the Stanford d.school

"Too many students ask, 'Why are we learning this?' This book offers a powerful answer: because the world needs your ideas, your voice, and your leadership. Rooted in decades of practice, this book proves that when project based learning is done well—and led well—it can be a force for justice, belonging, and breakthrough achievement. From district vision to classroom practice, *Project Based Learning for All* connects the dots with frameworks, examples, and leadership practices that feel both grounded and inspiring. It belongs on every education leader's desk."

—**Jeff Wetzler,** co-founder of Transcend, co-author of *Extraordinary Learning for All*, and author of *Ask: Tap into the Hidden Wisdom of People Around You*

"I wish this book had come out 14 years earlier!! After keynoting the first several PBL World conferences starting in 2012, I was approached by many school and district leaders—fired up about project based learning and full of big important questions: 'How do I help others see the power of PBL?' 'How do I build the culture, conditions, and capacity to spread and deepen PBL?' *If only I could have handed them this book* . . . It would have saved them so much time—and spared them my own far-less-comprehensive answers! I'm thrilled that today's and tomorrow's leaders now have this essential resource at their fingertips."

—**sam seidel**, co-author of *Hip Hop Genius 2.0* and *Creative Hustle*, co-editor of *From White Folks Who Teach in the Hood*, and K12 Lab Director of Strategy at the Stanford d.school

PROJECT BASED LEARNING FOR ALL

A Leader's Guide

BOB LENZ   LISA MIRELES
Foreword by Shane Safir

Arlington, Virginia USA

San Rafael, California USA

2111 Wilson Boulevard, Suite 300 • Arlington, VA 22201 USA
Phone: 800-933-2723 or 703-578-9600
Website: www.ascd.org • Email: member@ascd.org
Author guidelines: www.ascd.org/write

999 Fifth Avenue, Suite 200
San Rafael, CA 94901
www.pblworks.org

Richard Culatta, *Chief Executive Officer;* Anthony Rebora, *Chief Content Officer;* Genny Ostertag, *Managing Director, Book Acquisitions & Editing;* Bill Varner, *Senior Acquisitions Editor;* Mary Beth Nielsen, *Director, Book Editing;* Jennifer L. Morgan, *Editor;* Lisa Hill, *Graphic Designer;* Cynthia Stock, *Typesetter;* Kelly Marshall, *Production Manager;* Shajuan Martin, *E-Publishing Specialist*

Copyright © 2026 ASCD. All rights reserved. It is illegal to reproduce copies of this work in print or electronic format (including reproductions displayed on a secure intranet or stored in a retrieval system or other electronic storage device from which copies can be made or displayed) without the prior written permission of the publisher. By purchasing only authorized electronic or print editions and not participating in or encouraging piracy of copyrighted materials, you support the rights of authors and publishers. Readers who wish to reproduce or republish excerpts of this work in print or electronic format may do so for a small fee by contacting the Copyright Clearance Center (CCC), 222 Rosewood Dr., Danvers, MA 01923, USA (phone: 978-750-8400; fax: 978-646-8600; web: www.copyright.com). To inquire about site licensing options or any other reuse, contact ASCD Permissions at www.ascd.org/permissions or permissions@ascd.org. For a list of vendors authorized to license ASCD ebooks to institutions, see www.ascd.org/epubs. Send translation inquiries to translations@ascd.org.

ASCD® is a registered trademark of Association for Supervision and Curriculum Development. All other trademarks contained in this book are the property of, and reserved by, their respective owners, and are used for editorial and informational purposes only. No such use should be construed to imply sponsorship or endorsement of the book by the respective owners.

All web links in this book are correct as of the publication date below but may have become inactive or otherwise modified since that time. If you notice a deactivated or changed link, please email books@ascd.org with the words "Link Update" in the subject line. In your message, please specify the web link, the book title, and the page number on which the link appears.

PAPERBACK ISBN: 978-1-4166-3396-9   ASCD product #124033 m12/25
PDF EBOOK ISBN: 978-1-4166-3397-6; see Books in Print for other formats.
Quantity discounts are available: email programteam@ascd.org or call 800-933-2723, ext. 5773, or 703-575-5773. For desk copies, go to www.ascd.org/deskcopy.

ISTE+ASCD Member Book No. FY25-8. ISTE+ASCD mails member books quarterly (Jan–Mar, Apr–Jun, Jul–Sep, Oct–Dec) with 4 books to Enhanced members and 8 books to Pro members. For current details on membership, see www.iste-ascd.org/member-books.

Library of Congress Cataloging-in-Publication Data

Names: Lenz, Bob author | Mireles, Lisa author
Title: Project based learning for all : a leader's guide / Bob Lenz and
    Lisa Mireles.
Description: Arlington, Virginia, USA : ASCD, [2026] | Includes
    bibliographical references and index.
Identifiers: LCCN 2025025368 (print) | LCCN 2025025369 (ebook) | ISBN
    9781416633969 paperback | ISBN 9781416633976 pdf
Subjects: LCSH: Project method in teaching
Classification: LCC LB1027.43 .L457 2026 (print) | LCC LB1027.43 (ebook)
LC record available at https://lccn.loc.gov/2025025368
LC ebook record available at https://lccn.loc.gov/2025025369

35 34 33 32 31 30 29 28 27 26   1 2 3 4 5 6 7 8 9 10 11 12

PROJECT BASED LEARNING FOR ALL

Foreword by Shane Safir ix

Prologue xiii

1. Frameworks for Scaling High-Quality PBL for All Students 1
2. Reframing Leadership: Key Mindsets for Scaling Deeper Learning Using PBL 19
3. Crafting the Vision 30
4. Developing the Culture 46
5. Designing the Infrastructure 61
6. Building Capacity: Gold Standard PBL 83
7. Building Capacity: Assessing Deeper Learning 102
8. Measuring Impact for Continuous Improvement 118
9. Translating PBL Leadership Practices for District Leaders 139
10. Onward to Deeper Learning 159

Acknowledgments 167

Appendixes 169

References 207

Index 211

About the Authors 215

Foreword

I first encountered Bob Lenz in the summer of 1998 at a weeklong training in project based learning (PBL) for teachers. My choice of the word "encountered" rather than "met" is intentional—entering Bob's orbit was an encounter that altered my trajectory. Fresh out of my first year of teaching high school social studies, I was tired but excited to learn new methods. A week spent studying PBL through compelling project examples with Bob's wise guidance, followed by an invitation to dig in and design a project, blew up my entire paradigm for teaching in the best possible way. At the training, I joined forces with Lisa Arrastia, a brilliant educator at a nearby, affluent, independent school, whose context was as different as you can imagine from the large urban public high school where I was teaching. Together, we hatched a collaborative public–private school student investigation into educational equity in which our students worked together over several months, visited each other's schools, and ultimately presented their poetry, policy ideas, and voices to a large audience of family and community members. The project was featured in "Making the Grade," an award-winning episode of a public television documentary series (KQED, 1999). That experience changed me and remains to this day one of my top three professional experiences.

Bob went on to found the Envision Schools network, where I later had the privilege to provide leadership coaching for two of the schools profiled in this book: Impact Academy of Arts & Technology in Hayward, California, and Envision Academy of Arts & Technology in Oakland, California. These schools lived and breathed PBL and its close kin, performance-based assessment, in no small part because Bob was leading a *movement* birthing beautiful, dynamic communities of practice. I watched as teachers like Laureen Adams and leaders like Alcine Mumby brought PBL to life as a deeply student-centered, equity-driven strategy. In 2003, Bob's teachings and modeling had already influenced my own leadership as the founding co-principal of a small public high school, June Jordan School for Equity, in San Francisco, where we incorporated similar structures such as regular exhibitions of student learning, performance-based systems of student portfolios and defenses of work, and collaborative planning time for teams of teachers each week.

Bob Lenz and Lisa Mireles are the real deal, and they write from personal, experiential, and moral authority about the topic at hand. They have supported more than 3,000 school and district leaders across 60 districts committed to advancing deeper learning through PBL. The lessons for leaders inside this book have been hard-won, and the book truly delivers on its purpose: to provide educational leaders with a strategic road map to PBL implementation that is rooted in equity and ultimately transforms teaching and learning so that every learner can thrive. These authors make it clear that PBL is a strategy for operationalizing deeper learning for *all* children, particularly children at the margins. They don't shy away from naming the forces of systemic oppression and racism that PBL must and can disrupt when it's implemented with fidelity and strategic leadership. They define Gold Standard PBL with its seven Essential Project Design Elements and companion pedagogical practices. And they posit, from their wealth of knowledge and expertise, that "transformational leaders are the primary accelerators of change." As someone who has wrestled with and written about leadership in *The Listening Leader* (Safir, 2017) and *Street Data* (Safir & Dugan, 2021), I could not agree more.

So why is *Project Based Learning for All: A Leader's Guide* so important and timely?

First, it provides a road map to coherence at every level of the system. While many books treat pedagogy in isolation from leadership, or site leadership separate from district leadership, Bob and Lisa's book sees the forest *and* the trees. Throughout these pages, readers receive the gift of actionable frameworks like the PBL Equity Levers for teachers, school leaders, and district leaders and tools like the PBL Culture and Vision Elements and Leadership Practices. Practitioners at heart, the authors enact the best of adult learning theory by incorporating a Know, Do, and Reflect infrastructure into each chapter, as well as practice tips like "Replace a regular staff meeting with a teacher-driven exhibition where individuals or teacher teams share their projects with others" in a glow-and-grow format. Such a simple but transformative idea!

Second, *Project Based Learning for All* paints a much-needed picture of what "making PBL happen for all students" looks like. The authors not only draw on their own experiences and rich histories of leading and developing PBL-centered schools but also infuse powerful case studies from across the United States for a vivid composite depiction of PBL-centered school transformation. The result is a compelling invitation to dream big and act boldly.

Finally, this book provides abundant tools, protocols, and rubrics for leaders to self-assess their capacity for PBL leadership and move toward high-quality PBL implementation across their educational context. Bob and Lisa clearly understand that it's not just the technical work of "doing PBL" that matters, it's the complex, adaptive work of culture building. To that end, the book includes discussions of critical pivots for leaders to facilitate their shift from expert consultants to adaptive coaches.

In a moment where public education is being actively dismantled, Bob and Lisa help us envision a world in which school is meaningful and relevant for every learner while oriented toward empowering students at the margins—a reality in which students actively engage in their learning with their teachers, their peers, and ultimately, authentic audiences for their work. And in so doing, they give us hope and the tools to revive education for its greatest good, in service of thriving communities and healthy democracies.

Shane Safir
Founding co-principal, June Jordan School for Equity
Author, *The Listening Leader: Creating the
Conditions for Equitable School Transformation*
Co-author, *Street Data: A Next-Generation
Model for Equity, Pedagogy, and School Transformation*

Prologue

A High School Story

In the San Francisco Bay Area, students in a small network of charter schools for grades 6–12 benefit from a secondary education focused on producing graduates who meet the following criteria:

- They are qualified to attend a public university in California, having passed rigorous state university–approved courses.
- They have mastered a set of leadership skills such as critical thinking, collaboration, communication, and project completion.
- They have demonstrated their readiness for their next step in life (college and/or career) in a reflective portfolio of mastery-level work aligned to college readiness.
- They have defended their portfolio to a panel of teachers in front of their families and peers.

Ninety-five percent of students in these schools identify as Black or Brown. More than 75 percent qualify for free or reduced-price lunch and will be the first in their family to attend college. But the students defy several scholarly averages for Bay Area students of similar demographics. Ninety percent or more of them qualify to attend a California public university and are accepted to a four-year college. Equally important, if not more so, their college persistence rate (percentage of students who return to college for a second year) is 85 percent. Asked to identify the factors in their college success, former students name their experiences with project based learning as one of the top three; their teachers and the portfolio creation and defense process are the other two.

The schools lean heavily on project based learning (PBL) to support the development of academic knowledge, leadership skills, and self-reflection or metacognition in their learners. All community members understand how PBL and the rigorous work of portfolio preparation and defense prepare students for success in college, career, and family and community life.

An Elementary School Story

At a small elementary school in Hawai'i, students engage in multiple place-based projects each year. The projects are designed to connect authentically with the arts and to partner students with community members who provide content expertise and feedback to teachers and students. Most students work at or above grade level, give presentations on their projects for an adult audience multiple times a year, and are enthusiastic about learning. At graduation, each 6th grade student takes the stage and shares their learning journey with the entire community. They explain how and why they embody one of the school's core values and demonstrate their readiness for middle school.

Teachers have common planning time weekly and a full day each quarter to develop standards-aligned projects with one another and with specialty teachers in such areas as art, music, Hawaiian studies, marine science, and gardening. When designing and implementing projects, teachers consider their students' strengths, opportunities, interests, and passions. Additionally, projects align vertically across the grades to ensure the gradual deepening of critical academic skills. Staff regularly collaborate on examining student work, implementing protocols that ensure project quality. They also discuss how best to scaffold learning so students can make deeper connections. At this school, project based learning is not an "add-on"; instead, it is the heart and core of the student experience.

The Pathway to Deeper Learning

As you may already have guessed, these vignettes are based on our own school leadership experiences: Bob led Envision Education in California, and Lisa headed Kaua'i Pacific School in Hawai'i. These scenarios have several commonalities, but in each, the key to success rests in the commitment of leadership to practicing PBL as a pedagogical pathway to deeper learning for students. In addition, in both educational ecosystems, we needed to be relentless in our quest to create more open, dynamic, and equitable school structures and systems to honor and strengthen the innate genius and identities of everyone in the school community.

Although this book includes some of our own insights and experiences as PBL teachers and leaders, it is mostly a compilation of the many lessons we and our incredibly talented colleagues at PBLWorks have learned through working alongside transformational school leaders. The following chapters explore insights acquired over more than 30 years through the efforts of the Buck Institute for Education (doing business as PBLWorks), illustrated with examples from school leaders in our network, to illuminate the many reasons that educational leaders should work toward scaling high-quality PBL across their schools and districts, with all students benefiting from this deeper learning pedagogical approach.

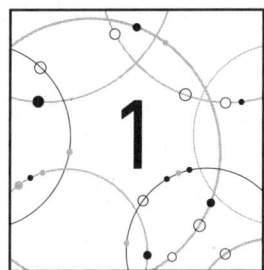

Frameworks for Scaling High-Quality PBL for All Students

You, a school leader, have likely picked up this book because you already know that project based learning (PBL) is a valuable and powerful educational tool, and you want to know what you can do to facilitate PBL in your educational context. PBL engages students, opens the doors to deeper learning, and fosters greater retention of content knowledge—why *wouldn't* we want to spread the practice as widely as possible? We recognize that the task of ensuring all of your students have access to deeper learning experiences may feel daunting. But we also believe fervently that, as you proceed through the book, you will not only gain knowledge and tools to support you on your journey toward PBL implementation across your school or district but also come to realize why ensuring deeper learning for all students should become a top priority for school leaders everywhere.

Deeper Learning for All

First, it is important to come to a shared understanding of what we mean by *deeper learning for all*. *Deeper learning* takes place when students develop and apply competencies needed to succeed in our rapidly evolving world. These competencies, often called success skills, typically include some combination of academic mindsets, self-directed learning, content expertise, collaboration, communication, creativity, critical thinking, and problem-solving skills (Hewlett Foundation, 2013).

To cultivate these competencies, students need learning environments that foster student agency, well-being, and co-construction of knowledge. Far too many schools still rely on industrial-age learning models that favor the transmission–acquisition approach. Leaders who want to ensure students are future-ready must take instructional approaches that intentionally and authentically link knowledge acquisition with the acquisition of specific success skills. Deeper learning combines the principles of knowledge transmission and co-construction, allowing students to explore and address complex interdisciplinary questions and challenges (Sliwka et al., 2024).

At its simplest, deeper learning engages students in learning core academic content and applying that knowledge to relevant and authentic real-world problems. Students in deeper learning classrooms actively engage in inquiry-based, hands-on learning to explore questions across the disciplines, developing well-supported arguments, creative solutions, and meaningful products. They strengthen their verbal, written, and visual communication through a variety of authentic tasks. Throughout the process, students build essential social-emotional skills such as perseverance, collaboration, resilience, and a growth mindset. They also leverage modern technologies to research, share knowledge, and connect with experts and peers around the globe. Their learning is showcased through authentic performance assessments that highlight what they know and can do in real-world contexts (Learning Policy Institute, n.d.). Deeper learning awakens the realization in students that they can be agents of positive social change.

The second part of the phrase—*for all*—emphasizes that deeper learning is beneficial for every student, especially those who are disengaged from or marginalized by traditional schooling. As an antidote to the traditional transmission–acquisition model that many students struggle with, PBL connects with students' interests and identities, provides a stronger "why" for learning, and fosters an asset-based approach to student strengths and needs. All students, regardless of their background, should have access to meaningful learning experiences that help them grow. We address the use of PBL to foster educational equity later in this chapter.

PBL Frameworks

We believe project based learning is not only the strongest pedagogical pathway to deeper learning but also a valuable tool for disrupting systemic oppression and racism. PBL actively engages students in authentic, personally meaningful learning, unleashing a contagious creative energy in both students and teachers. A growing body of research shows that PBL promotes student learning and may be more effective than traditional instruction in social studies, science, mathematics, and literacy (Duke et al., 2021; Kingston, 2018; Saavedra et al., 2021). With PBL, students work on a project over an extended period of time—from a week to a semester—that engages them in solving a real-world problem or answering a complex question. They demonstrate their knowledge and skills by creating a public product or presentation for an appropriate audience. As a result, students develop deep content knowledge as well as skills in critical thinking, collaboration, creativity, and communication.

Educational practitioners often use the terms deeper learning, PBL, Gold Standard PBL, and high-quality PBL (HQPBL) interchangeably—and this book does as well—but there are some specific characteristics to know about the latter two frameworks. The first, *Gold Standard PBL*, is a comprehensive, research-informed model developed by PBLWorks (Larmer et al., 2015). The framework encompasses two useful lenses to help curriculum designers center students' acquisition of key knowledge, understanding, and success skills (see Figure 1.1). The first lens applies seven Essential Project Design Elements to guide and support teachers in creating or adapting projects for optimal learning. The second identifies seven Project Based Teaching Practices that are critical to student success in a PBL classroom. When used together to focus PBL implementation, these lenses are powerful tools that help teachers, schools, and organizations improve, calibrate, and assess their practice, leading to deeper learning for students.

In response to the emergence of PBL models and frameworks that describe what *teachers* should be doing to plan and implement PBL effectively, the *HQPBL Framework* (HQPBL, n.d.) was developed to focus on the *student* experience with PBL and identify what makes that experience truly high quality. A lack of a shared, learner-centered vision of HQPBL

Figure 1.1 Gold Standard PBL Model

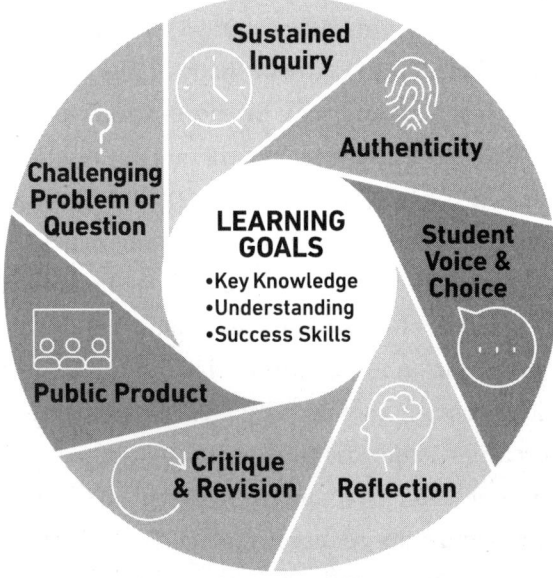

Copyright © 2019 Buck Institute for Education. Reprinted with permission.

makes it difficult for educators to know how to use PBL to improve student experiences, learning, and development. PBLWorks (then the Buck Institute for Education, or BIE) took the lead to engage with partners worldwide to tackle this challenge. With the support of the William and Flora Hewlett Foundation and the Project Management Institute for Education Foundation, the steering committee and advisory board determined that HQPBL experiences must include the following elements:

- Intellectual challenge and accomplishment
- Authenticity
- Public product
- Collaboration
- Project management
- Reflection

The framework includes a set of indicators for each element to help inform and improve project design and implementation.

Because we are committed to the idea that all PBL experiences should be high quality and meet the criteria for the Gold Standard PBL Framework, this book uses HQPBL, PBL, and Gold Standard PBL interchangeably. Applying these qualifications to PBL in the classroom will lead to deeper learning for all students.

Now that we have clarified definitions and introduced frameworks, we turn to some of the justifications and theories behind our approach to PBL implementation.

PBL as a Lever for Equity

Years ago, when Bob first embarked on his journey with PBL, he achieved a great deal of success at his predominantly white, middle-class, suburban high school. But he was nonplussed when visitors from less advantaged schools would remark, "This would never work with my students"—and many of our PBLWorks colleagues have had similar experiences. These skeptical reactions propelled Bob to branch out to more racially and socioeconomically diverse areas in the San Francisco Bay Area when co-founding Envision Schools. He was determined to show that PBL could help students thrive in any classroom in any school—and he did. Compared with their suburban peers, Envision students qualify for state universities at a higher rate, are accepted to four-year colleges at a higher rate, and show a higher rate of college persistence (returning to college for a second year) (Envision Education, n.d.).

We know that PBL can be an effective pedagogical approach to disrupting systemic oppression and racism. To that end, the entire PBLWorks community crafted a statement on our Racial Equity Imperative (see Figure 1.2). Our vision, focus, and commitment have been shaped and refined by the National Faculty, the entire PBLWorks staff, the racial equity action team, and the PBLWorks board of directors. As we move to action, we will continue to revisit and refine our stance and vision for our work toward racial equity in education.

PBL leaders need to prioritize communicating with colleagues and the community about the connections between PBL, deeper learning,

Figure 1.2 PBLWorks Racial Equity Imperative

Our Vision for Racial Equity

Racial equity for all students will be achieved when race and ethnicity no longer predict the outcome of a young person's educational future. The board, leadership team, PBLWorks staff, and National Faculty commit to identifying and dismantling racial inequities and providing equity-based support so that students furthest from opportunity can achieve their full potential.

Our Focus on Racial Equity

Project based learning (PBL) enables all students—especially Black and Brown* students—to gain the academic content knowledge and understanding, the success skills, and the sense of agency that will help them in college, career, and life.

Given systemic and institutionalized racism and the oppression of Black and Brown students in the educational system, we strive individually and collectively to ensure that Black and Brown students experience Gold Standard PBL at least twice a year in their school.

Our focus on advancing racial equity for Black and Brown students does not preclude us from addressing any and all other issues of inequity and oppression for any other people and working for all students to experience Gold Standard PBL at least twice a year. Furthermore, we work toward *all students* experiencing Gold Standard PBL—excluding no one.

We envision a world in which race, ethnicity, and other aspects of identity do not predict the outcomes or opportunities available to young people. And we know that Gold Standard PBL, when implemented with an intentional focus on equity, is one powerful way to work toward this vision.

*A note about our use of "Black and Brown": Our use of the term "Black and Brown" is meant to include students with heritage or familial association from the African diaspora, First Nations, Latinx, Southeast Asian, Native Hawaiian, Pacific Islanders, Middle Eastern, and many others.

Copyright © 2020 Buck Institute for Education. Reprinted with permission.

and educational equity. An intentional focus on equity matters, especially when we are all working hard to push against what author and activist bell hooks calls "the narrow boundaries that have shaped the way knowledge is shared in the classroom" (1994, p. 44).

PBLWorks[1] has been on our own multiyear journey to advance racial equity because we knew that we needed to engage in this work as an organization before we could authentically address it with our partners. As part of this work, we have been exploring the question "What are the specific mindsets and priorities that PBL teachers and leaders can leverage to provide equity-centered, meaningful learning experiences for all students?" To ensure that implementing PBL leads to more inclusive and equitable learning experiences and outcomes for all students and adults, we developed the list of PBL Equity Levers explored in Figure 1.3.

These levers amplify the power of the Essential Project Design Elements and Project Based Teaching Practices to reach all learners. They are intended to provide a starting point for teachers and leaders to consider when designing or developing projects and plans. Because equity work is an ongoing process rooted in curiosity and reflection at all system levels, the figure supplies guiding questions for teachers, school leaders, and district leaders. Let's unpack each equity lever to help you understand exactly how PBL can support your efforts to center equity in your leadership and your school.

Knowledge of Students

For teachers, this lever relates to the authentic ways we get to know our students, their families, and their communities to ensure that the projects in our classrooms are relevant to students' lives and rooted in a meaningful context. It includes bringing an asset-based lens to our work with students, knowing each student well enough to be able to see and build on the unique gifts they bring into the classroom. It also includes teaching a historically accurate and inclusive curriculum that addresses the intellectual legacies of Black and Brown students: "the fact that people who look like them created much of the knowledge base of today's world" (Delpit & Dowdy, 2008, p. 41).

Knowing students well requires staying curious about their needs so you can effectively address any barriers preventing them from accessing

---

[1] A version of this discussion on equity levers through page 10 also appeared in "4 Equity Levers in Project Based Learning" (Field, 2021).

Figure 1.3 PBL Equity Levers

Equity Lever	Teachers	School Leaders	District Leaders
Knowledge of Students Students engage in projects that capture their interests, honor their strengths and identities, and meet their needs.	How can I learn about (and build meaningful relationships with) my students so that I can design and facilitate projects that capture their interests, honor their strengths and identities, and meet their needs?	How can I learn about (and build meaningful relationships with) my teachers to facilitate professional learning that captures their interests, honors their strengths and identities, and meets their needs?	How can I learn about (and build meaningful relationships with) my school leaders to better support them on their PBL journey?
Cognitive Demand Students are engaged in intellectually challenging work, know their teachers believe in them, and have appropriate supports that advance their academic mindset and cognitive growth.	How can I hold high intellectual expectations and provide appropriate support for all students to advance each student's academic mindset and cognitive growth?	How can I hold high expectations and provide appropriate resources for all teachers to support them in using Gold Standard PBL to advance each student's academic mindset and cognitive growth?	How can I hold high expectations and provide appropriate support for all leaders to advance each leader's PBL mindset and growth in understanding and supporting Gold Standard PBL?
Literacy Students engage in experiences that deepen their capacity to read, write, listen, and speak across various contexts and disciplines.	How can I provide experiences that deepen students' capacity to read, write, listen, and speak across various contexts and disciplines?	How can I provide experiences that deepen teachers' capacity to use literacy practices within Gold Standard PBL across various contexts and disciplines?	How can I provide experiences that deepen leaders' ability to support teachers in strengthening literacy using Gold Standard PBL?
Shared Power Students experience student voice, choice, agency, and interdependence in their classroom.	How do I cultivate student voice, choice, agency, and interdependence in our classroom?	How do I cultivate teacher and student voice, choice, agency, and interdependence in our school?	How do I cultivate leader voice, choice, agency, and interdependence across our district?

Copyright © 2021 Buck Institute for Education. Reprinted with permission.

learning. This lever also requires introspection from us as educators—including the perspectives, cultural lenses, and biases we each carry—as we consider how our identities and experiences shape how we connect with our students.

For this lever to come to life in classrooms, leaders need to model what it looks like by getting to know teachers authentically and ensuring that professional learning includes experiences relevant to your teachers' current reality and context. As a leader, you also need to bring an asset-based lens to your work with teachers to see and build upon their unique gifts, as well as reflect on your own perspectives, cultural lenses, and biases.

Cognitive Demand

Cognitive demand relates to providing rigorous challenge and appropriate support to all learners so that every student is engaged in meaningful and complex intellectual work. It involves building what Zaretta Hammond calls "learning partnerships" with students so that they persist through challenges and develop a sense of their own efficacy as learners (Hammond, 2015). An intentional focus on cognitive demand is critical to countering racialized disparities in teacher expectations for student learning.

To support this lever, you should hold high expectations for teachers when it comes to implementing PBL and provide the support and conditions needed for them to do so effectively. This means building learning partnerships with teachers and co-designing professional learning opportunities and structures that empower teachers to persist through implementation challenges and develop a sense of efficacy in leading PBL with their students.

Literacy

Literacy is an equity issue (Sedita, 2020), and researchers maintain that effective PBL can support students' literacy development (Duke et al., 2021). Projects can provide rich and authentic opportunities to build literacy skills and incorporate meaningful scaffolds that help students engage in reading, writing, listening, and speaking for a variety of purposes and audiences.

When it comes to this lever, consider how you might strengthen teachers' ability to integrate literacy practices into their project design and daily teaching practice. Addressing such topics as text-based protocols, vocabulary building techniques, and writing strategies in the context of PBL-focused professional development sessions can strengthen teachers' understanding of how to weave literacy instruction into their PBL practice.

Shared Power

Shifting our instructional approach to a collaborative, learner-centered model can redistribute power in the classroom. Equity-centered PBL classrooms shift the dynamics among students and teachers from "power over" to "power with." Teachers learn alongside students, and when possible and appropriate, students play an active role in shaping their own learning, leading to the realization that supporting one another's learning, growth, and belonging is mutually beneficial.

To promote the concept of students and teachers sharing power and learning alongside each other in equity-centered classrooms, it's vital that you share power with and learn PBL alongside your teachers. You must cultivate teacher and student voice, choice, agency, and interdependence in your school to manifest a collaborative, learner-centered model that redistributes power at the school level. This might mean that you provide as much opportunity as possible for teachers to shape their own PBL-focused professional learning and that you consider where and how you can distribute decision-making to those closest to the work.

Although PBLWorks has made progress on our organizational equity journey and our ability to center equity in our work with teachers and leaders, this is a never-ending journey. For example, as we revisit our design, teaching, and success skills rubrics descriptors, our racial equity action teams are actively asking themselves tough questions about the intersections of PBL, social justice, educational equity, and racial equity. Our goal is to interrupt oppressive systemic inertia in favor of liberation and love for every member of each educational ecosystem.

Leaders as Accelerators

Becoming a school leader is a journey that requires fortitude, humility, courage, and most of all, love. Becoming a school leader who takes the additional step to embrace deeper learning to amplify the identities, power, and agency of those they work with is not for the faint of heart. Leading for deeper learning requires leaders to recognize that the cornerstone of effective school leadership centers around the willingness to embrace vulnerability and to regularly reflect on the daily lessons that come from interactions with other educational leaders, the community, teachers, and most importantly, students. One recent study suggests that leaders with a clear transformational leadership style are likely the only leaders with the foresight necessary to drive change to foster deeper learning (Sliwka et al., 2024). Jayson Richardson and colleagues (Richardson et al., 2021) unpack this with their "Portrait of a Deeper Learning Leader," which includes living the vision, authenticity, agency in learning, trusting teachers as professionals, openness to new approaches, overcommunicating change, restlessness toward equity, and courage to challenge norms.

In 2021, the Wallace Foundation published *How Principals Affect Students and Schools*, a synthesis of 20 years of evidence of the impacts of school leadership (Grissom et al., 2021). The research report concludes that effective school leaders influence not only student achievement but also crafting schools' visions, building positive school culture, and engaging with and supporting teachers in their professional learning. However, we know that school leaders often forgo leadership development opportunities so that teachers can benefit from a school's limited resources to pursue classroom-focused professional learning.

In our work with schools and districts across the country, we have learned firsthand that transformational leaders are the primary accelerators of change. We are writing this book to help you on your own transformational journey to becoming a PBL leader. Focusing on the school leader as a change driver is critical to achieving more sustained and equitable practices that positively influence student outcomes.

Leadership Theory of Action

Over the years, we have worked with hundreds of insightful and courageous school leaders who put PBL at the heart of their change efforts. These leaders have played a vital role in helping us to develop and refine our Leadership Theory of Action, depicted in Figure 1.4. The PBLWorks Leadership Theory of Action reflects our collective experience and research-informed belief that implementing high-quality PBL effectively starts with developing transformational leaders. Leaders who demonstrate

Figure 1.4 PBLWorks Leadership Theory of Action

LEADERSHIP	SCHOOL CONDITIONS	TEACHER PRACTICE	STUDENT EXPERIENCE	STUDENT OUTCOMES
Leaders demonstrate specific knowledge, skills, practices, and dispositions and put specific structures in place so that . . .	Key conditions related to vision, culture, capacity building, and continuous improvement exist for effective implementation of high-quality PBL so that . . .	Teachers design or adapt Gold Standard PBL units and implement Gold Standard PBL Project Based Teaching Practices so that . . .	All students experience at least two projects that meet the criteria for high-quality PBL so that . . .	Students demonstrate the academic knowledge, success skills, and student empowerment outcomes described in the graduate profile.

Copyright © 2019 Buck Institute for Education. Reprinted with permission.

a specific set of PBL knowledge, skills, practices, and dispositions and put specific structures in place to meet critical conditions for deeper learning are the catalyst for improved student outcomes across the school. Given the importance of leadership as an accelerator of change, our goal is for this book to serve as a helpful and practical toolbox to help you lead PBL implementation for the benefit of all of your students.

Holonomy and Symmetry

Although we wholeheartedly believe that we must start with school leaders, we also understand that leaders are situated within complex, interdependent educational ecosystems. Thus, we embrace the importance of understanding and leaning into *holonomy*—the science of interacting parts within wholes—to achieve improved outcomes for all students. In this context, it refers to the principle that the parts of a system (in this case, individuals within the educational system) can only be fully understood in relation to the whole system and vice versa. Costa and colleagues' (2014) view of holonomy in education integrates individual autonomy with collective responsibility, emphasizing the interconnectedness and alignment of all participants in the educational process.

At the most basic level, holonomy means that if we want systemic change, all layers of the system must model and reflect the behaviors we want to see in students in the classroom. In other words, symmetry matters. If we want students to engage in Gold Standard PBL, then leaders need to ensure that teachers experience professional learning and work environments that model and reflect the Gold Standard PBL Essential Project Design Elements and Project Based Teaching Practices. If we want students to become self-directed learners, then leaders must create conditions for our teachers to be self-directed. If we want teachers to shift from a "sage on the stage" to a more learner-centered "engage and coach" practice, then leaders must model and reflect the same. As such, when we refer to deeper learning for all, we mean for *every student, teacher, leader, and community member* in the educational ecosystem. Let's unpack this further by exploring our Strategic Leadership Framework.

Strategic Leadership Framework

Since 2017, PBLWorks has served more than 3,000 school and district leaders in 60 districts committed to advancing deeper learning through PBL. The PBLWorks Strategic Framework (Figure 1.5) is the cornerstone of our work with districts nationwide. Our nested approach reflects the concept of holonomy, starting with students at the center and working outward, resulting in a holistic, aligned approach to student learning on four levels:

1. Ensure students experience high-quality project based learning (HQPBL) and collect *evidence* of learning.
2. Develop the *capacity* of teachers to create HQPBL learning experiences using our Gold Standard PBL frameworks.
3. Develop the capacity of school leaders to create the *conditions* and structures necessary to support teachers in implementing Gold Standard PBL so students experience HQPBL.
4. Develop the capacity of system leaders (district administrators, curriculum and instructional coaches) to build *coherence* and the required infrastructure to support and sustain schools' implementation of HQPBL.

Figure 1.5 PBLWorks Strategic Leadership Framework

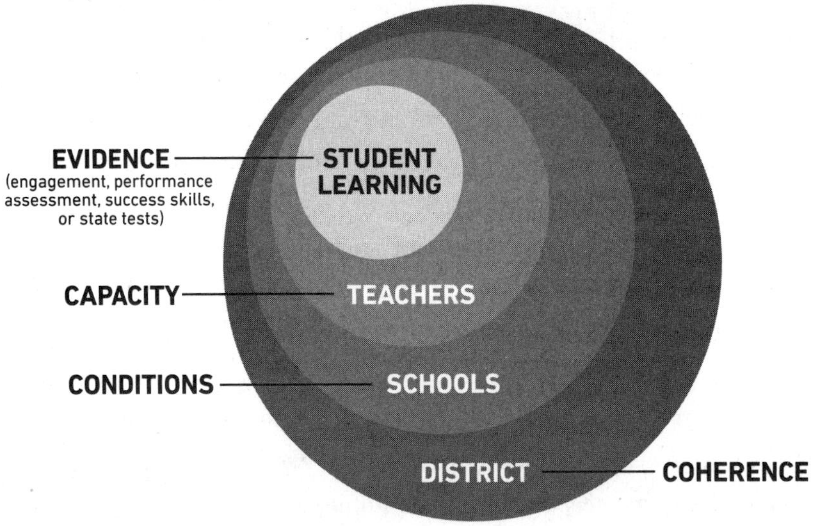

- EVIDENCE (engagement, performance assessment, success skills, or state tests) — STUDENT LEARNING
- CAPACITY — TEACHERS
- CONDITIONS — SCHOOLS
- DISTRICT — COHERENCE

Copyright © 2019 Buck Institute for Education. Reprinted with permission.

To be sustainable, any innovation, including PBL, must place student learning at the core and be designed to affect all levels of the system. Increasing teachers' capacity to implement PBL at the classroom level can positively and equitably improve student learning experiences and outcomes. Teachers, in turn, require supportive conditions at the school level from their school leaders. District leaders must support school leaders and establish coherence, priorities, and high expectations for systemwide change.

This work starts by aligning and centering shared aspirations for student learning outcomes. Once we have identified what students need to know and be able to do, we use the Gold Standard PBL frameworks to support school leaders in building their understanding of and rationale for implementing PBL so they can help teachers do the same. We work with district leaders to build their understanding of Gold Standard PBL so they can make connections, build coherence, and support school leaders by using our model. Along the way, we work with teachers and leaders to move from planning to doing as quickly as possible for two reasons: (1) we want them to experience some PBL quick wins, and (2) we know from experience that the doing will inform the planning.

District Logic Model

Within the Strategic Leadership Framework, our professional learning and outcomes for teachers, school leaders, and district leaders reflect our District Logic Model, which encompasses four key domains: vision, culture, capacity building, and continuous improvement (Figure 1.6). Connecting and transcending all four domains requires teachers, school leaders, and district leaders to work individually and collectively to build an infrastructure that includes the critical conditions necessary for PBL to thrive across the system.

While we recognize that systemic change is complex and that school and district leaders must attend to all four domains all the time, we have learned that it is helpful for leaders to consider the domains and infrastructure individually and tackle the leadership practices within each domain in a particular order. Thus, we have organized the heart of the book to follow that progression. Chapters 3–8 explore the leadership practices associated with vision, culture, infrastructure, capacity building, and continuous improvement in detail. We encourage you to work through the book in the order that makes the most sense for you, although if you are new to the work, you might find it best to work straight through the

Figure 1.6 PBLWorks District Logic Model

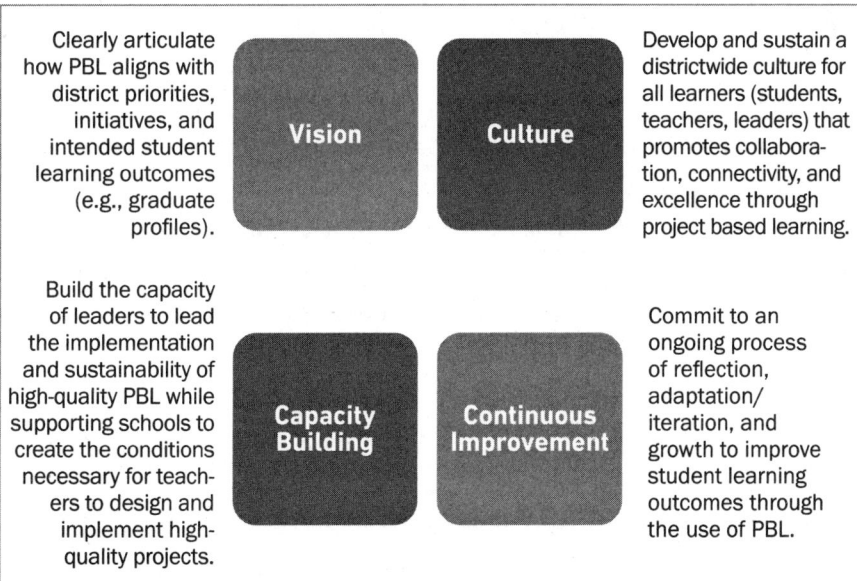

Copyright © 2019 Buck Institute for Education. Reprinted with permission.

chapters. If you are more experienced with the work and are grappling with a particular area (e.g., finding time for teachers to plan), start with the chapter that addresses that (e.g., Chapter 5, "Designing the Infrastructure"). Do what works for you and your school! Following are some brief descriptions of the content covered in each chapter.

Crafting the Vision (Chapter 3). Craft a clear vision for your classroom, school, or district that includes Gold Standard PBL to help all students, especially those who face systemic oppression, gain the knowledge and skills they need to adapt, flourish, and contribute to a changing world.

Developing the Culture (Chapter 4). Develop and sustain a class-, school-, and districtwide culture that promotes Gold Standard PBL as a vehicle for advancing deeper learning outcomes, social-emotional learning, and equity.

Designing the Infrastructure (Chapter 5). Design the classroom, school, and district infrastructure and conditions needed to implement Gold Standard PBL effectively and sustainably.

Building Capacity: Gold Standard PBL (Chapter 6). Build teacher and leader capacity to implement high-quality PBL projects that advance and accelerate learning for all students, and build the capacity of school and district leaders to support teachers with PBL implementation.

Building Capacity: Assessing Deeper Learning (Chapter 7). Build teacher and leader capacity to create and use a high-quality performance assessment system that includes aligned formative and summative assessments of crucial knowledge, understanding, and success skills.

Measuring Impact for Continuous Improvement (Chapter 8). Build more holistic classroom, school, and district systems to measure and share the stories of the impact of PBL and an ongoing process of reflection, adaptation, and growth to improve student learning.

Translating PBL Leadership Practices for District Leaders (Chapter 9) provides additional and specific guidance for district leaders to understand better their unique role in supporting schools by building coherence and creating systemwide support for school leaders on their PBL journey.

And finally, in **Onward to Deeper Learning (Chapter 10),** we encourage you to reflect on themes addressed throughout the book and initiate your action plan for implementing PBL in your school context with your colleagues.

Relentless Reflection

We share a deep respect and appreciation for the love that educational leaders bring daily to an incredibly challenging role in an increasingly complex world. We hope you connect to the practices we share and can see a path toward making them your own. We also hope you will see yourselves in some of the stories shared. Most importantly, we hope you are inspired to joyfully try new things—practices that might take you out of your comfort zone—to create more equitable, supportive, deeper learning communities. To that end, we designed this book to be a tool for reflection as well as a guide to PBL implementation.

We are strong proponents of using the *Know–Do–Reflect (KDR) framework* in our work, and we use this instructional framework as an organizing scheme for Chapters 2–9. Each chapter starts with a *Know* section that includes some theoretical and conceptual background about the domain emphasized in the chapter and describes the leadership practices associated with the domain and how they are applied in schools and classrooms. We also share leadership stories from the field of how one of our partners brought PBL-focused practices to life in their own context.

Once you deeply understand the domain and associated practices, you will move on to the *Do* section, which features suggestions for leadership moves (mini-trials) you can put into action related to the knowledge you've just acquired. Finally, the *Reflect* section includes prompts to reflect on what you learned during your mini-trial and through consuming the content of the chapter to help you close the gap between your current and envisioned leadership practices in the focus domain.

Using the KDR instructional framework as a lens to examine our own school leadership experiences, we estimate that we spent at least 85 percent of our time focused on knowing and doing during the school day. With little time for reflecting, we missed out on being able to pause for serious thought and reflection on our leadership.

It takes intentional and conscious effort to understand how you lead, why you lead the way you do, and the impact of your leadership (as well as the impact of your past school experiences and current school culture on you). Without taking time to reflect, your leadership is likely driven by mindsets you've adopted by default.

Do these words ring true for you? Are you leading a school that looks like the school(s) you attended? Is your school led in a way you would want the school your children attend to be led? If you could create a school from scratch, would it look like the one you lead?

Consider the following questions as you weigh the value of relentless reflection:

- What's the balance of KDR in your leadership?
- When was the last time you had a chance to reflect deeply on your leadership?
- How regularly do you create space for reflection in your practice?
- How consistent have you been in making that happen?

Many leaders view change as a series of steps or separate components, rather than as an integrated process that involves adjustment and adaptation. We encourage you to be selective with the guidance this book provides. Modify the ideas shared throughout based on your unique school context. Reflect on what you learn in each chapter by physically writing responses to the reflection prompts interspersed throughout the text (in fact, we encourage you to have a journal just for this purpose). You know your learners, teachers, and community best, and you are the best person to lead them on this fulfilling and educational PBL journey.

Chapter 2 explores the mental models and mindsets that are most conducive to implementing and supporting high-quality PBL in schools and classrooms. It's a good place to start.

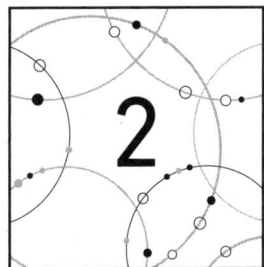

Reframing Leadership: Key Mindsets for Scaling Deeper Learning Using PBL

Mindsets and Mental Models

Providing more intellectually challenging, meaningful, relevant, engaging, and deeper learning to all students requires school leaders to think in new and different ways, which in turn requires examining and upgrading your mindset (i.e., attitudes and beliefs). Your mindset drives how you think, learn, and behave—in short, how you lead and live your life. Research has provided definitive evidence that our mindset can shape our own and others' motivation and learning (Dweck & Leggett, 1988). This has important implications for school leaders, particularly those of us who commit to engaging all students, especially Black and Brown students, in deeper learning.

KNOW

As we think about mindset, it's important to understand the influence of mental models on our beliefs. The term "mental models" had already been established in 1943 by Kenneth Craik, but Peter Senge brought it into wider use in the first edition of his remarkable book *The Fifth Discipline* (Senge, 1990). Simply put, he says, "Mental models are deeply ingrained assumptions, generalizations, or even pictures or images that influence how we understand the world and how we take action" (p. 8). He further explains mental models using an iceberg metaphor: Our actions are the observable part of the iceberg, just the tip; submerged below the water level are the actual causes of those actions. Mental models sustain, shape, and create our behaviors (even if unconsciously).

Senge proposes the following:

> The discipline of working with mental models starts with turning the mirror inward; learning to unearth our internal pictures of the world, to bring them to the surface and hold them rigorously to scrutiny. It also includes the ability to carry on "learningful" conversations that balance inquiry and advocacy, where people expose their own thinking effectively and make that thinking open to the influence of others. (2006, pp. 8–9)

He suggests that if you want to be an effective transformational leader, you must know yourself and your biases, understand how your perceptions and experiences shape reality, find people to triangulate your views with, and approach those conversations with openness.

The biggest challenge in implementing good design ideas in any organization is navigating existing beliefs and countering the tendency of stakeholders to assume and generalize—in other words, transforming the organization's mental model. Leaders need to have the inquiry and advocacy skills to minimize the gap between the theory espoused and the theory in use.

Mindsets and their underlying mental models are powerful. Simply put by Henry Ford, "Whether you believe you can do a thing or not, you are right." As a school leader, you can tremendously influence culture, climate, teaching, learning, and student outcomes at your school. We believe that. Do you? Your position provides a unique opportunity to make significant positive impacts on students, educators, families, and even communities. Transformation is the ultimate expression of school leadership. From our experience, it takes work to uncover and examine our mindsets and make necessary shifts to create new learning environments and experiences. This is especially important for those of us who have been socialized in traditional public schools and have internalized mindsets that unconsciously drive our thinking, behaviors, and leadership.

Traditional education mindsets assume that the current way of "doing school" is intractable and immutable. From our experience and that of our partners in the field, we know otherwise. Reframing how we feel and think about our leadership and education in general is fundamental to transformation. We believe that three essential leadership mindset shifts can create conditions in which all students, especially Black and Brown students, engage in deeper learning to achieve success in college, career, and life:

- Build capacity in others by building your own leadership capacity.
- Focus on both "here and now" and "there and later."
- Target simultaneous, correlated outcomes.

> **Reflect**
>
> **Consider a recent initiative you led that went well. What mindsets did you need to develop or influence to lead the change?**

Build Capacity in Others by Building Your Own Leadership Capacity

The first mindset shift requires some initial self-assessment. How do you stay current with your own learning? When was the last time you sat down and looked deeply at your leadership in terms of strengths and areas for growth? How much time have you spent developing your leadership in the last year? The last two years? The last five years? How does that compare with the time, energy, and resources that you spend developing capacity in your teachers and staff? If your experiences are anything like ours, finding time for and justifying spending resources on your own professional learning is a challenge.

The struggle is real. Take, for example, 2020 results from a survey of principals conducted by the National Association of Elementary School Principals (NAESP) and the Learning Policy Institute, in which 84 percent of respondents faced obstacles to engaging in professional development. They further identified lack of time (67 percent), lack of coverage for their absence from the building (43 percent), and lack of money (42 percent) as limitations on their efforts (Levin et al., 2020).

In our experience, it's countercultural for leaders to invest in their own professional learning. You might wonder how you can justify spending funding on your own leadership development when teachers are spending their hard-earned money on classroom materials. Or how you can step away from the building when there are so many day-to-day needs to address. But we ask, how can you justify *not* investing resources in your leadership? As the Wallace Foundation reports, "It is difficult to envision an investment with a higher ceiling on its potential return than a successful effort to improve principal leadership" (Grissom et al., 2021, p. 43). Making any fundamental and lasting changes to schooling, including implementing project based learning for all students, requires a level of leadership beyond traditional teacher education and administrator licensing coursework and day-to-day experiences.

Building your own leadership capacity is a necessary first step to building capacity in your teachers and students. For us, it's no different than putting on your oxygen mask first on an airplane before assisting others. If you run out of oxygen, you can't help anyone else; if you have not built your own capacity, you cannot fully support teachers in building theirs. Your instructional leadership is essential to your school's success.

Investing in yourself will help you better understand why this work is right for your school. Build your own understanding of what PBL is and isn't and how it can help you achieve your vision for all students. In our experience, this investment is one of the best gifts you can give your teachers because your knowledge and understanding will set the stage for deep and sustained PBL implementation.

We'll explore this further in Chapter 6, "Building Capacity: Gold Standard PBL"; share what we've done at PBLWorks; give examples of how school leaders in our network develop their capacity and their teachers; and give you more opportunities to reflect on how you think about building capacity in your schools.

> **Reflect**
>
> **How might you build or strengthen your own knowledge of PBL as an instructional approach so that you can play a key role in building the capacity of others to engage in this work?**

Focus on Both "Here and Now" and "There and Later"

We know firsthand how the overwhelming demands related to everything from safety to academic success can consume all of a school leader's time and energy. Everyday school leadership typically focuses on "putting out fires" and managing whatever is happening in the moment—attending to the "here and now."

Jackson Hole (Wyoming) High School Principal Scott Crisp, an ambassador fellow for the U.S. Department of Education in 2017, shared a snapshot from his professional life:

> The day of the principal can be both predictable and chaotic. My role requires the ability to situationally pivot on the fly to meet the immediate needs of students, parents, faculty, and other stakeholders. I must be sensitive to a variety of immediate and long-term demands while simultaneously balancing the interests and beliefs of the school community. (Crisp, 2017, para. 8)

School leaders are often so focused on putting out daily fires that they can't see the moves they need to make from a broader perspective. To lead for deeper learning, you need to step away and analyze the entire situation from a strategic point of view. In other words, you need to keep your vision—the "there and later"—in your mind's eye as you work to achieve it.

Senge (1990) describes the gap between a leader's vision and the current reality as a source of energy or "creative tension" that needs to be managed. Because we are acutely aware of the differences between where we are now and where we would like to be, such a gap can make our vision seem unrealistic or fanciful. We might become discouraged or feel hopeless.

However, the tension between the ideal state and our present state can also be a source of energy. Figure 2.1 depicts this tension as a rubber band stretched vertically between two planes representing the vision and the current reality. If there were no distance between the planes, there would be no need to take action to move toward the vision.

To relieve this creative tension, we can either decrease our expectations or change our reality to approach our vision. It's important to remember that the plane that is entirely under our control—the vision—can be scaled back if necessary to deal with emotional tension, or discouragement (Senge, 1990). But ridding ourselves of uncomfortable feelings comes at the cost of abandoning our true aspirations.

Figure 2.1 Creative Tension

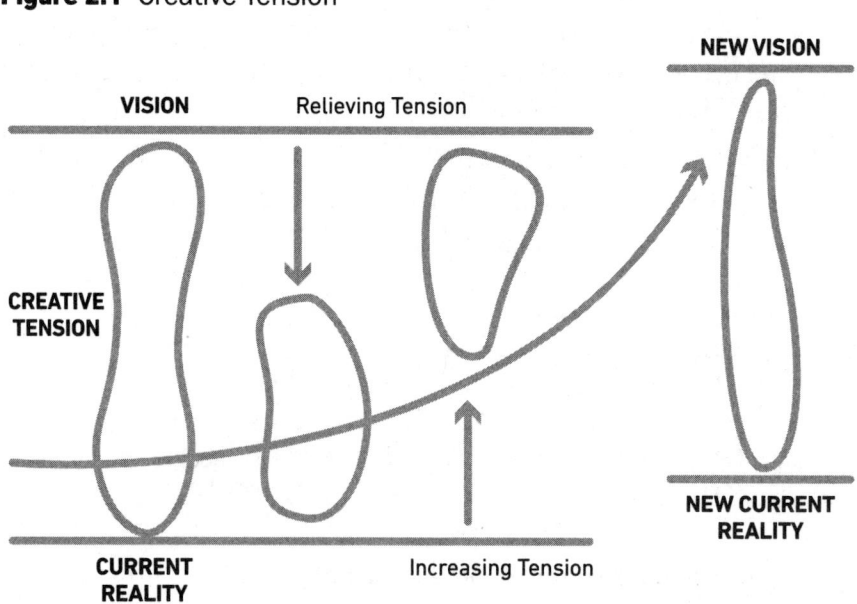

Source: From *Generative Scribing: A Social Art of the 21st Century* (p. 129), by K. Bird, 2018, Pi Press. Reprinted with permission.

Managing a school's current reality requires a lot of time, energy, and emotional resources from school leaders, and making significant changes to promote deeper learning is even more demanding. As a leader who wants to transform learning, you must have an eye on both the "here and now" and the "there and later"—and invest time and energy to move from one to the other. Attempting to focus on both perspectives at once may seem contradictory, but we contend that the efforts can and must coexist. As we say at PBLWorks, it is tension to hold—not a problem to solve.

> **Reflect**
>
> **How might you carve out space (daily or weekly) to focus more on both the "here and now" and "there and later"? How can you dedicate protected time to determining how to get "there" quicker?**

Target Simultaneous, Correlated Outcomes

Across the country, standardized test scores are upheld as a yardstick for students, teachers, schools, and districts. Having to focus instruction on the contents of these tests continues to put educators in a bind because we know that success in today's world depends on students developing academic, social-emotional, and success skills—characteristics best fostered by a whole-child approach to education. To achieve the simultaneous outcomes of specific knowledge acquisition and broader skill development, we turn to deeper learning and PBL.

Deeper learning improves multiple student outcomes, including attendance, engagement, academic skills, creativity, critical thinking, collaboration, communication, and self-directed learning. The nested shapes in Figure 2.2 illustrate how PBL units meet subject-area content standards while also allowing students to learn disciplinary dispositions (e.g., thinking like a scientist) and develop other proficiencies such as lifelong learning and personal agency.

Further supporting the need to shift from single-metric targets to simultaneous outcomes, a series of reports from the American Institutes for Research (AIR) (Bitter et al., 2014; Huberman et al., 2014; Zeiser et al., 2014) provide a comprehensive look at schools practicing deeper learning strategies, including PBL. In a quasi-experimental proof-of-concept study, AIR investigated whether schools in a network described as a Deeper Learning Community of Practice achieved better student outcomes than local comparison schools. Here are some highlights from AIR's Study of Deeper Learning: Opportunities and Outcomes:

- Students who attended network schools graduated on time at statistically significantly higher rates.
- After graduation, students who attended network schools were more likely to attend a four-year college and enroll in more selective institutions.

Figure 2.2 Simultaneous Outcomes

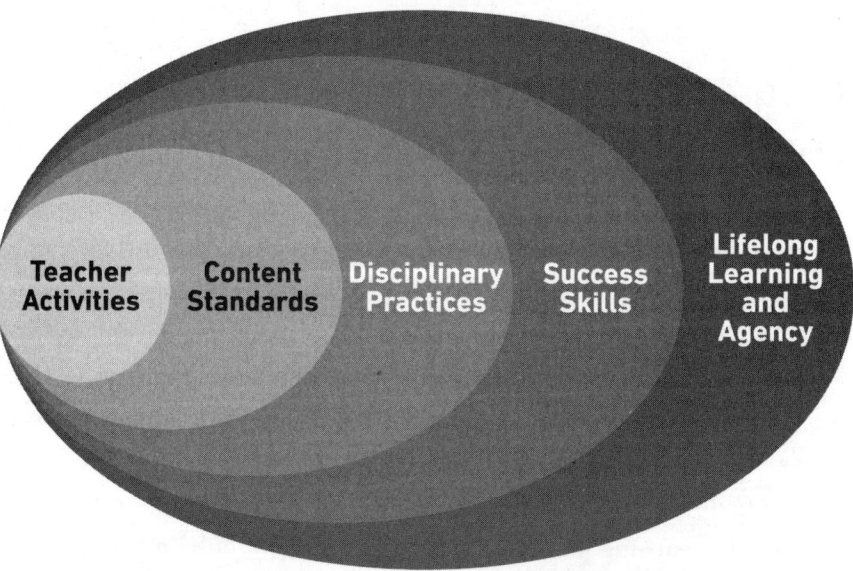

Copyright © 2024 Buck Institute for Education. Reprinted with permission.

- Students who attended network schools achieved higher standardized test scores on both state assessments and international tests measuring core content knowledge and complex problem-solving skills.
- Students who attended network schools reported higher levels of academic engagement, collaboration skills, motivation to learn, and self-efficacy.
- While in school, students who attended network schools benefited from greater opportunities for deeper learning through such practices as PBL, internship opportunities, and longer-term cumulative assessments.
- Attending a network school benefited diverse groups of students. Regardless of background or incoming achievement levels, students who attended network schools achieved the same positive deeper learning outcomes. (Huberman et al., 2014; Yang et al., 2016; Zeiser et al., 2014; Zeiser et al., 2016)

Perhaps two of the study's most significant findings are the development of higher levels of academic engagement, collaboration, motivation, and self-efficacy and the success of deeper learning practices regardless of student income levels or prior school achievement (Huberman et al., 2014). AIR's research helps dismantle the myth that deeper learning only works for advantaged, already achieving students. On the contrary, deeper learning strategies give all learners opportunities, experiences, and skills each of us wants for our children.

Reflect

What are some correlated outcomes that matter to you? Are you measuring and monitoring them? If not, how might you? If you are, what are you learning, and how might you share that knowledge with others?

Our mindset shapes how we make sense of our leadership role and understand what is possible for ourselves, our teachers, our students, and our communities. Mindset theory suggests that how we view our capabilities, talents, and intelligence influences the way we live our lives and how we pursue our goals—whether we give up when faced with failure or respond with more effort and dedication (Gottfredson & Reina, 2020). Focusing on supporting these three key mindset shifts in yourself and your teachers will better equip you for success on your PBL leadership journey.

Reframing Your Mindset in Practice

Consider how you can apply your new knowledge on reframing leadership mindsets to promote deeper learning for all of your students. Here are some ideas:

- Keep a professional learning journal documenting how much time you devote to and what activities you engage in to further your own professional development. Monitor these activities for a week or even a month.
- Learn something new or reflect on the last new thing you learned. Exploring concepts from the perspective of a novice can help you remember what it's like to engage in knowledge or skill acquisition that pushes you out of your comfort zone. How did it feel? What mindset did you need to be successful? How does the experience connect to the mindset shifts outlined in this chapter?
- Carve out 5 to 10 minutes daily or 30 to 45 minutes weekly to focus on the "there and later"—your vision for implementing deeper learning in your school. Make a list of one to three moves you can take to get you "there." Hold yourself accountable for making those moves.
- List all the outcomes you use to determine student success and examine the list critically. How many outcomes are traditional or one-dimensional? How many are correlated with each other or multidimensional? To what extent do these indicators tell you the true story of student learning at your school? What might need to change as you implement deeper learning practices?

Final Reflections

1. What did you try? What did you learn from your experience?
2. How has reading this chapter shifted your understanding of mindsets and the need to shift away from traditional mindsets in education?
3. List one to three quick actions you can take to build your capacity for PBL, leverage creative tension, and advocate for simultaneous, correlated outcomes in your professional context.

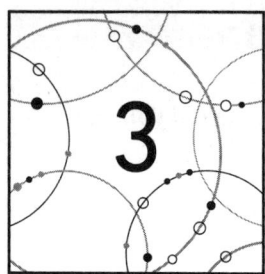

Crafting the Vision

*When people come together around common vision,
they can accomplish great things. We need the instruments
that pull our people together, not apart.*

—Nainoa Thompson, Pwo navigator and CEO,
Polynesian Voyaging Society

With any journey, you need to know where you want to end up. Even if you don't know exactly how you'll get there, you must begin by determining your destination. An educational leadership journey such as the one you're embarking on often targets as its destination a graduate profile that embodies the skills students should have when they move on from the school or district. But defining the specifics of such a profile demands an honest assessment of your starting point. What do your current graduates look like? What skills do they take to college or the workforce? Once you've established your origin, you can determine where you want to go by crafting a graduate profile that highlights the knowledge, skills, and dispositions you aim for all students to embody. This may seem like a simple concept, but it's rarely explicitly stated or properly implemented.

> **Reflect**
>
> **What is your mental model for developing your school's vision for PBL? What does it look like, sound like, or feel like?**

There are two aspects to shaping your plans into a compelling vision: They must be crystal clear, and they must be communicated as a story. In his book *The Wayfinders*, Wade Davis (2009) shares an example of the power of vision from the Polynesian Voyaging Society (PVS) and Nainoa Thompson, its legendary leader. Since 1976, the *Hōkūle'a* canoe has sailed the Pacific Ocean and across the globe using Indigenous practices of wayfinding by stars and observing nature. The PVS, Thompson, and *Hōkūle'a* have created a shared vision of a renaissance for Hawaiians, Polynesians, and Indigenous people everywhere.

> In 1999, having crisscrossed the Pacific from Marquesas [Islands] to Aotearoa [Māori name for New Zealand], the Polynesian Voyaging Society embarked on its most ambitious journey. With Nainoa as navigator, the *Hōkūle'a* would try to pull Rapa Nui [native name for Easter Island] out of the sea. It was a wildly ambitious expedition. The distance from Hawaii to Easter Island is roughly 10,000 kilometers, but the journey implies crossing the Doldrums and tacking into the wind for 2,300 kilometers, which effectively doubles the total sailing distance to nearly 20,000 kilometers. And all to make landfall on an island 23 kilometers in diameter, less than a single degree on a compass, had in fact a compass been on board.... At one point, close to their goal, Nainoa snapped awake

in a daze and realized that with the overcast skies and the sea fog, he had no idea where they were. He had lost the continuity of mind and memory essential to survival at sea. He masked his fear from the crew and in despair remembered his teacher, Mau's, words. *Can you see the image of the island in your mind?* He became calm, and realized that he had already found the island. It was the *Hōkūle'a*, and he had everything he needed on board the sacred canoe. Suddenly, the sky brightened and a beam of warm light appeared on his shoulder. The clouds cleared and he followed that beam directly to the island of Rapa Nui. (Davis, 2009, pp. 62–63)

Consider Mau's question to Nainoa. Can you see the image of your graduates in your mind? What do they know? What can they do? How do they reflect on and transfer their learning to new and different situations? Research—and our experience—tell us that clearly visualizing the future state of your school and student learning makes achieving your goals far more likely (Cheema & Bagchi, 2011).

At PBLWorks, we try to walk the walk. We crafted a short, compelling vision for our work to spread PBL:

> We envision that all students, especially Black and Brown students, engage in high-quality project based learning to deepen their learning and to achieve success in college, career, and life.

This vision statement is our North Star, which guides our strategies and the specific work we do to build the capacity of educators, teachers, and leaders to make great projects happen for every student.

In our work with leaders, we help them elucidate their North Star with the following steps:

- *Develop a clear vision* that describes student outcomes for success in college, career, and life for all students, especially those who are historically marginalized or underserved.
- *Commit to Gold Standard PBL* and articulate how it will serve students and align with other school initiatives.
- *Advocate for all students* to engage in Gold Standard PBL with high expectations and support for their success.

Figure 3.1 lists four elements that leaders should consider when creating and sharing a PBL vision. Each element has an associated leadership practice that leaders should demonstrate to accelerate the full realization of the vision.

Figure 3.1 Crafting a PBL Vision: Elements and Leadership Practices

Element	Leadership Practice
Deeper learning competencies Rating: _____	I ensure that all students in my school engage in projects that include deeper learning competencies and are aligned to deeper learning outcomes.
Personal and shared vision Rating: _____	I led or am leading dialogue with my school community about how PBL aligns with our school vision.
Advocacy for students Rating: _____	I engage teachers and community members in sustained dialogue about how PBL and deeper learning support all students to learn at high levels and serve to diminish achievement and opportunity gaps.
Commitment to PBL Rating: _____	I am committed to leading my school to use PBL to help achieve deeper learning outcomes for all students, including those furthest from opportunity.

On a scale of 1 ("I have not yet explored this") to 4 ("This is central to my practice"), rate yourself on each leadership practice to evaluate your current reality and recognize where you need to focus your efforts.

After you've read the chapter, use the space below to reflect on what concrete steps you can take to further develop your PBL vision in your educational context.

Copyright © 2018 Buck Institute for Education. Reprinted with permission.

Deeper Learning Competencies

Across the United States, school districts and even states are working with parents, teachers, students, and community members to create "portraits" of their graduates. (We've shared some examples in Figure 3.2.) These profiles encapsulate the knowledge, skills, and dispositions students will possess at the end of their schooling—qualities supported by the deeper learning competencies illustrated in Figure 3.3. This process of envisioning what future graduates will know and can do provides a direct connection to the value of implementing PBL schoolwide, and that implementation begins with you, the leader.

When we work with schools or districts to develop their vision, we often start with a modified chalk talk protocol we call the Ideal Graduate exercise. We ask participants to create a profile of their ideal graduate by responding to the following prompts:

- What does your ideal graduate know or believe about themselves as learners or learning in general?
- What are the things they can do? What knowledge, skills, or dispositions do they have?
- What does your ideal graduate care about?

Figure 3.2 Example Graduate Profiles

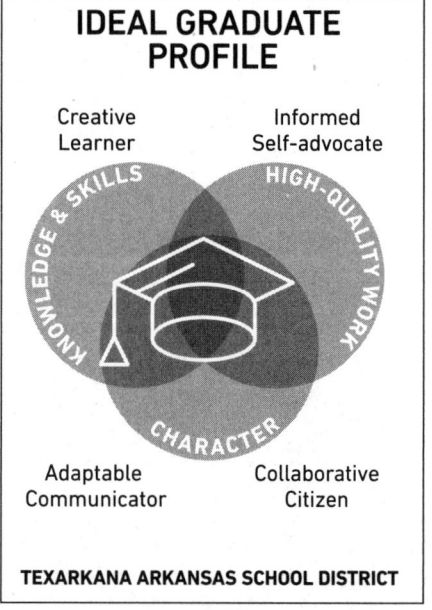

Source: University Prep Schools, Detroit, MI, and Texarkana Arkansas School District. Reprinted with permission.

Figure 3.3 Deeper Learning Competencies

CONTENT EXPERTISE
Students develop key competencies, skills, and dispositions with ample opportunities to apply knowledge and engage in work that matters to them.

CRITICAL THINKING & PROBLEM SOLVING
Students consider a variety of innovative deeper learning approaches to address and understand complex questions that are authentic and important to their communities.

COLLABORATION
Students co-design projects with peers, exercise shared decision-making, strengthen relational agency, resolve conflict, and assume leadership roles.

EFFECTIVE COMMUNICATION
Students practice listening to understand, communicating with empathy, and sharing their learning through exhibiting, presenting, and reflecting on their work.

SELF-DIRECTED LEARNING
Students use teacher and peer feedback and self-reflection to monitor and direct their own learning while building self-knowledge both in and out of the classroom.

ACADEMIC MINDSET
Students establish a sense of place, identity, and belonging to increase self-efficacy while engaging in critical reflection and action.

Source: High Tech High Graduate School of Education. Reprinted with permission.

From there, we invite participants to silently collaborate on a poster titled "Our Ideal Graduate." (If the group size is over 10, we divide them among a few posters). Working in silence not only allows everyone to freely express themselves without interruption but also gives them time to reflect and consider other points of view before commenting. Participants gather around, adding words or images representing the ideal graduate. They are encouraged to silently connect ideas using symbols or images. Once the contributions slow down, we invite participants to review their work and then engage in a discussion prompted by any or all of the following questions:

- What do you notice about our poster(s)?
- What does our ideal graduate tell us about what we value?
- What does the profile tell us about what our students need?
- What else is coming up for you?

This discussion is key to developing a vision for student outcomes and laying the groundwork for achieving them.

Consider what qualities would be displayed in a graduate portrait for your school or district. As you begin, you might find it helpful to do the following:

- *Reflect* on where and how students currently demonstrate evidence of deeper learning competencies.
- *Review graduate profiles* from other schools to see how yours compares. Do they include deeper learning competencies such as collaboration, critical thinking, creativity, communication, and self-directed learning? If your school or district had already developed a profile of a graduate, review it with key opinion leaders on campus to ensure it reflects these qualities.
- *Share a PBLWorks project video* (e.g., the Water Quality Project video at https://bit.ly/projectvids) in a staff meeting and ask staff to reflect on and discuss the extent to which students in the video demonstrate the deeper learning competencies.

Personal and Shared Vision

The first question we ask school and district leaders we work with to uncover their vision for their students is "Why PBL?" If the leaders themselves cannot articulate a clear reason for implementing high-quality project based learning, how will their teachers, students, and parents understand the advantages to making such a big change?

Leaders often respond that they are looking to increase student engagement—especially post-pandemic—or make school more fun. Sometimes they are pursuing professional development in PBL because of our good reputation among teachers. These reasons are valid; PBL is more engaging, and teachers highly value learner-centered, applicable, respectful professional development. Nevertheless, we encourage the leaders we work with to reflect and create a vision that both follows our KDR framework and clearly states the desired learning outcomes for their students based on project based learning as a primary strategy and methodology. Next, they reflect on their personal vision for PBL, ensure it aligns with the school or district's vision, and make a plan for creating a shared vision.

Once you are clear on your own vision for PBL and can explain how it fits into the school or district's vision, you can begin essential conversations with key stakeholders to help them better understand the combining of these visions. Start with your leadership team, teachers, students, advisory board, parents, or other community members. Engaging in a project experience or unpacking your school or district's graduate profile can spark meaningful conversations and connect you with the hopes and aspirations of your school community.

We have also found that the most effective leaders tell compelling stories about what it looks and sounds like when students demonstrate the benefits of PBL in their community, especially if the students are from marginalized backgrounds or overlooked by typical education practices. Often, storytellers contrast the current reality—the "here and now"—to the vision—the "there and later" to articulate arguments in favor of PBL implementation. This emotional connection through storytelling can be enormously beneficial as you launch the change process.

Bear in mind that even those whose hearts are ready to embrace the change may ask, "How do we know this will work? What is the evidence?" As the leader, you must be ready to answer these essential questions. Your thoughtful response will give teachers who may be resistant to change the data they need to understand the strong evidence supporting this approach. Fortunately, you don't have to reinvent the wheel in this regard. PBLWorks has worked with partner organizations, schools, and districts to create a substantial evidence base regarding the strengths of project based learning, available at www.pblworks.org/research/publications.

Lucas Education Research has also compiled a collection of peer-reviewed materials analyzing the effects of PBL (www.lucasedresearch.org/research), including the results of a randomized controlled trial designed to measure the impact of a project based learning approach to AP U.S. Government and Politics and AP Environmental Science courses in five mid- to large-size urban districts nationwide. In this study, not only did students achieve higher scores on an assessment for critical thinking and communication skills, but they also achieved better results on the official AP exams—8 points higher in the first year, and 10 points higher in the second. In addition, students from families of both lower and higher socioeconomic statuses saw improved performance on the exams (Saavedra et al., 2021).

As you develop both a personal and a shared vision for PBL, you might find it helpful to take the following steps:

- *Reflect* upon your own "why" for PBL.
- *Engage staff, students, and community members* in a mini-project to experience PBL from a student's perspective.
- *Understand the evidence supporting PBL* as a pedagogical approach that can improve student outcomes.
- *Develop a compelling elevator pitch or story* that explains "why PBL" and share with stakeholders.

Advocacy for Students

We sometimes hear school or district leaders say something like, "We can't do PBL with this group of students [most often Black and Brown students] because their basic skills are too low. Instead, we'll begin our implementation with the higher-achieving students and later roll it out to the rest, when their skills are more developed." The problem is that "later" rarely comes.

As a leader promoting PBL and deeper learning competencies, you must advocate for all students, especially marginalized students, to engage in Gold Standard PBL at least twice a year. Research supports this stance; recall that in Chapter 2, we shared the findings from the AIR study that showed that deeper learning practices had a positive impact on graduation rates, college-going rates, and standardized test scores. Regardless of background or incoming achievement levels, students engaged in deeper learning and achieved the same positive outcomes (Bitter et al., 2014; Huberman et al., 2014; Zeiser et al., 2014).

Schools must provide access to such instructional methods to *all* students during the school day so that every student can experience the joy of deep learning, master complex academic and social challenges, and discover their interests and passions. More privileged students may be able to access these rich experiences outside of school, but not everyone has the resources to do so. Consequently, we view PBL as an imperative for all students—especially Black and Brown students. In Figure 1.2, we shared PBLWorks's Racial Equity Imperative, which both inspires us and holds us accountable. We encourage you to review it and consider the extent to which you and your school community are committed to equitable outcomes for all students.

In our work with leaders, we build their capacity to advocate for all students. We model how to examine and discuss PBL research findings through structured protocols and encourage leaders to do the same with their staff and community members. Additionally, we invite school leaders to examine their own PBL implementation and outcome data using an equity lens to unpack and discuss the data. Finally, we ask leaders about the percentage of students in their school or district engaging in at least two PBL projects a year and support them in determining the best way to ensure that *all* of their students, regardless of perceived academic achievement level or need, have equitable access to PBL.

Here are some suggestions for expanding your work in student advocacy related to PBL:

- *Survey your staff* to see who is implementing PBL. Determine if there are any gaps in access at any grade level or for any subgroup of students.
- *Reflect on structures or policies* at your school that prevent certain students from accessing PBL. For example, in some schools, students working below grade level are offered remediation during the same block that other students are offered "enrichment." In other schools, English language learners are pulled out of core classes during PBL time.
- *Ask staff to reflect* on and share their most significant learning experiences, listening for common attributes or characteristics. Follow up by asking staff to consider how they can collectively ensure that all of their students experience significant learning.

Commitment to PBL

Like most educational changes—and changes in general—leading your school to begin to implement PBL is challenging. Most of this chapter has been about getting started with your school's vision and crafting a story that will compel teachers, parents, students, and community members to join you on this journey.

But it's essential that you remain committed to the practice even after the excitement of beginning the journey. After the initial launch and a wave of positivity, it's likely that you'll see a "dip" in enthusiasm. Like most education interventions, the outcomes from using PBL will take time to achieve. Meanwhile, teachers will struggle with the new teaching practices, students will push back on having to work through the inquiry themselves instead of relying on teachers to be the center of all knowledge and know-how, and parents will question whether their students are really learning anything.

PBL leaders need to stay committed to the plan throughout this trough. Continue to communicate the story of your vision for student learning and share your graduate profile aspirations. Provide resources and support for your teachers. Look for and shine the light on bright spots in the classrooms. Hold tight to the fact that PBL will improve teaching and learning for all of your students. When leaders are unwavering in their commitment to PBL, schools succeed with PBL.

We know all this is easier said than done. It's common to get distracted by new initiatives and expectations that inevitably arise. Effective PBL leaders become experts at connecting the dots between PBL and other initiatives. For example, if social-emotional learning (SEL) becomes a priority for your district, you can articulate how PBL develops SEL competencies (Lucas Education Research has written a beautiful white paper outlining the connections [Baines et al., 2021]). PBL can support and strengthen nearly every type of initiative you can think of—STEM, AI, assessment, literacy, Advancement via Individual Determination (AVID), and career and technical education, to name just a few. As a leader, you need to know and understand PBL deeply to build coherence and help teachers and other key stakeholders understand that PBL isn't one more thing to put on their plates. Instead, it can be the central container for a myriad of initiatives. Over and over in our networks, we see how committing to PBL pays off in ways you can't even imagine. Once the students complete their first project and public presentation of learning, the joy of PBL experienced by teachers, students, and parents will provide momentum for the journey.

Here are some tips to help you strengthen your commitment to PBL:

- *Talk to students* who attend a PBL school (or your own students) and ask them to share their experiences with you and your staff. PBL student panels offer compelling stories and evidence of how PBL changes lives.
- *Connect with other leaders* already on the PBL journey and those interested in walking alongside you on yours. Mentors, peers, and allies are invaluable when the going gets tough.

We hope you better understand how to craft your vision for PBL in your school and why having a North Star for this work is essential. The four elements and leadership practices associated with vision are deeply interconnected. Crafting a compelling vision for PBL requires developing a graduate profile that clearly names deeper learning competencies, developing your personal vision for PBL, and engaging in ongoing stakeholder conversations to build a shared vision for PBL. Additionally, consider showing how PBL aligns with other school initiatives and be sure to serve as the lead advocate for every student to experience Gold Standard PBL projects to ensure more equitable outcomes. The key to success will rest in the strength of your commitment to PBL as demonstrated by your actions. This will inspire others to strengthen their commitment.

Let's turn to a case study to learn how one leader crafted their vision for PBL in their school by focusing on advocacy for students.

Leadership Story: Advocacy for Students

On this blustery, crisp fall day in Brookline, Massachusetts, there is a powerful sense of inquiry at each table full of teams from schools belonging to the PBLWorks Massachusetts School Leader Network (MA SLN). One team is from Ivy Street School, an out-of-district therapeutic school that serves students from more than 25 districts in and around Boston. The Ivy Street team analyzes student project work samples using a research-based success skills rubric defining critical thinking. They are excited and energized about the progress their students have made and are deep in conversation about ways to continue to pave the path for students for the next school year and the future.

The idea of examining student work with a focus on critical thinking might not seem particularly innovative to many school leaders. What makes this story special, however, is the way the Ivy Street community has focused on their vision of advocating for students and achieving deeper learning outcomes for all students, including those who have typically been overlooked. Ivy Street's mission and vision are a clear example of advocating for students and building a culture of achievement for all:

> Using a lens of disability justice, we support the whole child through a person-first model driven by collaboration, a willingness to think big,

and a commitment to really knowing the people we work with. In our work with each youth, we start with their own "why"—and we allow healing and learning to grow from there. (Ivy Street School, n.d., para. 5)

Ivy Street frames its diverse student population—50 percent Black and Brown students and 100 percent students with disabilities, including over 50 percent of students with two or more high-needs disabilities—as an asset and connects it to their vision of educational equity and excellence for all. The school's emphasis on inclusion and advocacy is also reflected in the makeup of the PBL leadership team: administrators, educators, and related service providers working toward a personal and shared vision for PBL implementation.

The Ivy Street team's application to the MA SLN showed their clear commitment to implementing PBL as a path to deeper learning. They approached the work holistically, training all teachers and service providers. As Director of Related Services Emma Weiner articulated, "By incorporating service providers into project based learning at Ivy Street, providers were able to offer additional opportunities for sustained inquiry, more flexibility for student voice and choice, and more eyes and ears for revision and critique."

Advocating for students at Ivy Street has led to positive student outcomes. A key component to realizing their vision has been a focus on continuous improvement. All students had access to a PBL project in the first year of implementation. Examples of projects include students crafting a political campaign slogan and creating solar panels to learn about sustainable energy. Teacher survey data add to the story of schoolwide PBL support, with over 65 percent of teachers reporting that their projects included six to eight of the Gold Standard PBL Essential Project Design Elements.

Other findings, such as evidence of critical thinking in 50 percent of student work samples, have helped the team stay the course and identify new trails. Ivy Street has centered student voices and street-level data points to identify celebrations and joy in their work (for more on street data, see Safir, 2017, 2019). The importance of vision is embedded throughout the Ivy Street community. One student reflected on a project around creating a vision statement for their community: "Personally, I learned that even though not everything in a vision statement comes true, it's still important to have one because it's always essential to look at the future and address citizens' concerns."

Kate Garrity, chief learning officer for the school, summed up Ivy Street's approach to their vision for their students' educational journey:

> In order to best advocate for students' needs, a school team needs to be aligned in their vision for student success. The development of this vision should come from a multi- or interdisciplinary team that can take a whole-person vantage point for the skills, environment, and learning methods that meet each student where they are in their education journey. It is vital that the vision holds up from a top-down and bottom-up perspective, ensuring that the day-to-day supports a student receives align with the broader goals for all graduates, and that the broader goals also align with how the supports and accommodations for each student play out during their school days.

Crafting the Vision in Practice

To help you put your new knowledge into practice, here are some mini-trials you can use to explore what it's like to craft a vision for PBL. We encourage you to try at least one. Afterward, record your reflections and note any new insights you acquired.

- *Re-examine your school's vision statement* to ensure it aligns with your graduate profile. If you don't yet have a graduate profile, determine the degree to which the vision statement aligns with deeper learning competencies and consider the implications of where it agrees and where it diverges.
- *Develop a compelling three- to five-minute elevator pitch, video, or presentation* that shares your "why" for PBL. Remember to appeal to the heart and the mind.
- *Find out how your teachers feel about PBL.* You can administer a simple survey that addresses their willingness to try PBL, asking them to choose among statements such as "I am already doing PBL," "I am willing to try PBL," and "I am unwilling to try PBL."
- *Conduct the Ideal Graduate exercise* described on page 34, either individually or with a team of colleagues.

Reflect

What did you try? What did you learn from your experience?

How has your view of your role in shaping your school's vision for PBL shifted?

What are one to three actions you can take for quick wins to craft the vision you desire and need to advance PBL successfully in your context?

Final Reflections

1. Revisit your original mental model of developing your school's vision. How does it connect to what you have read in this chapter about crafting a vision for PBL? Did your thinking change at all? If so, in what ways?
2. Refer back to Figure 3.1. Using the same 1–4 rating scale, with 1 being "I have not yet explored this" and 4 being "This is central to my practice," how do you rate yourself now? What are your strengths? Where are your opportunities to grow?
3. What specific aspects of your current vision align with the elements of a PBL-focused vision? How might you expand on or strengthen these?
4. Who are your opinion leaders on campus? How might they help you develop and share your vision for PBL in your school?
5. Review the leadership story shared in this chapter. In what ways did Ivy Street School build their vision for PBL? What lessons could you apply in your setting or practice?

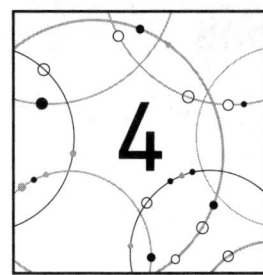

4

Developing the Culture

We need to create cultures that value and nurture agency. We must amplify the powerful voices of students and educators alike, and truly listen to them.

—Virgel Hammonds, CEO, Aurora Institute; PBLWorks Board chair

Visitors to PBL classrooms and schools often describe witnessing a buzz of activity, a sense of warmth among staff and between teachers and students, and a feeling of joyful energy. Students demonstrate pride in their work, and observers can sense that teachers trust students to drive their own learning. This commonality of culture is no accident—and it's no small part of implementing PBL successfully.

Our work with schools has taught us that doing PBL well builds a supportive culture, but if you don't concentrate on nurturing that culture, it will be hard to do PBL well. It is in the *doing*—the process of implementing project based learning—that the culture gets built. Co-creating agreements, being clear about what "good" looks like, engaging in critique and revision, and "doing good work together" build trust, care, teamwork, and agency and help you bring your PBL vision to life.

Educational leaders need to plan how to intentionally sustain a school- or districtwide culture that promotes Gold Standard PBL as a vehicle for advancing excellence and equity in student outcomes. In *Connecting the Dots: Teacher Effectiveness and Deeper Professional Learning*

(Bellanca, 2016), Lillian Hsu and Tim McNamara capture this idea beautifully: "The work we ask teachers to do—build relationships with members of the diverse school community, design authentic and engaging projects, and reflect on their work to improve—requires that we create an environment conducive to this work" (p. 303).

> **Reflect**
> **What is your current mental model of school culture? What does it look like, sound like, or feel like?**

Fostering a culture supportive of PBL depends on five key elements. Figure 4.1 lists these elements and their associated leadership practices. After you review the figure, conduct a self-assessment on how well your current practice incorporates the elements.

Student Agency

Student agency means that students truly believe that their voices matter and that they can make authentic choices and decisions to drive their learning. Student voice and choice is one of the Seven Essential Project Design Elements. We want students to feel seen, heard, and understood. They should know where to find the information they need to make their next move and where to turn when unsure about what to do next. Most importantly, they should feel trusted to advocate for themselves and others and be celebrated when they do so.

If we want students to feel seen, heard, and understood, we must ensure that teachers feel the same. Teachers with agency are more likely to foster student agency in their classrooms (Brandt, 2024). Think about how teachers exhibit agency in your educational setting. Do you ask them for feedback on your leadership or have them lead faculty meetings? How do teachers make decisions about what and how they are learning? How

Figure 4.1 PBL Culture: Elements and Leadership Practices

Element	Leadership Practice
Student agency Rating: _____	In my work as an instructional leader, I regularly look for and talk with teachers about student voice and choice in the classroom.
Risk-taking, trust, and growth Rating: _____	I have implemented regular and ongoing practices encouraging growth for all students and teachers, risk-taking, learning from failure, trust, reflection, and constructive critique.
Collaboration and shared responsibility Rating: _____	I ensure that teachers regularly collaborate to design and plan Gold Standard PBL and deeper learning and provide one another with feedback on practice and the rigor and quality of the projects they implement.
Making work visible Rating: _____	Learning presentations led by students and adults are a regular event, with the community invited to participate and presentations connected to community needs.
Celebrating success Rating: _____	I regularly recognize and celebrate teachers and students for achieving deeper learning outcomes, especially when that work advances equity in student outcomes.

On a scale of 1 ("I have not yet explored this") to 4 ("This is central to my practice"), rate yourself on each leadership practice to evaluate your current reality and recognize where you need to focus your efforts.

After you've read the chapter, use the space below to reflect on what concrete steps you can take to promote a culture supportive of PBL for all students in your educational context.

Copyright © 2016 Buck Institute for Education. Reprinted with permission.

about what they are teaching and how they drive student learning? To what extent do teachers feel safe, seen, and supported in their work or when they encounter challenges with their PBL practice? What avenues exist for them to advocate for their needs?

We encourage you to regularly observe teachers and talk with them about the level of student and teacher voice and choice in the classroom in a way that is authentic and comes from a place of love and connection. Once you better understand your current reality, your next steps to amplify student (and teacher) agency will likely become obvious. Here are some suggestions for beginning your assessment of student agency in your setting:

- *Walk through classrooms* regularly and conduct observations, focus groups, and surveys to understand better the various ways students are experiencing voice and choice in their classrooms. This can be done formally or informally.
- *Co-create shared agreements* and expectations for implementing PBL.
- *Model voice and choice* for your teachers by asking for input on and providing choices for the content and structure of PBL professional learning.

Risk-Taking, Trust, and Growth

In a PBL classroom or school, students and teachers feel safe and trusted to take risks. They feel encouraged to try new things and to devise new practices in service of their own growth. As a leader, you need to value growth and process/progress as much as, if not more than, outcomes. Learning from failure, reflection, and constructive critique should be the norm rather than the exception—for both students and teachers.

Effective PBL leaders understand that becoming a Gold Standard PBL practitioner involves high levels of vulnerability. When increasing the reach of PBL in your setting, you are effectively asking teachers to rethink what and how they teach. Many teachers are extremely proud of their practice, and their personal identity is wrapped up in these things. Learning to design and implement Gold Standard PBL projects requires teachers to reconsider how they build culture; engage and coach students; and assess, scaffold, and manage student interactions throughout a project.

Their current strategies might transfer, but it's likely they will have to stretch themselves. Smart PBL leaders meet teachers where they are and help them accept that they might not get PBL right the first time they try it. Consider trying the following to encourage risk-taking, trust, and growth:

- *Open meetings with check-ins and/or team-building activities* that get people out of their comfort zone while building trust.
- *Create safe spaces* to share successes and failures. We are strong proponents of Learning Circles, small groups of staff/teachers (or students) that stay together for a quarter, semester, or year. They come together regularly for check-ins that start with a silent pause to reflect on a short inspirational piece (e.g., quote, video, poem, reading, story), followed by individual journaling and a structured discussion protocol where each person has two uninterrupted minutes to share their thoughts. While each person shares, the others practice constructivist listening: listening for the benefit of the speaker rather than themselves.
- *Make space for regular and ongoing reflection.* We encourage PBL leaders to regularly ask three key questions when they visit classrooms or check in with teachers:
  - How's it going?
  - What are you learning?
  - What are your next steps?

Several things happen when you make intentional moves focused on risk-taking, trust, and growth. First, you gain deep insight into what teachers need to advance their practice. Second, you start to build a sense of trust with your teachers. Finally, both you and the teachers become more reflective and collaborative practitioners.

Collaboration and Shared Responsibility

Collaboration and shared responsibility are hallmarks of Gold Standard PBL. As a leader, you have to think about how to support teachers in practicing these skills so that they can replicate their experiences with their students. It's important for teachers to realize that "all our students are *all* our students," which means that they share responsibility for more than just the students in their classrooms, actively supporting one another and drawing upon colleagues' expertise to improve practice. To allow your team to fully realize opportunities for rich collaboration and shared responsibility, dedicate time and space for them to do the following:

- *Develop and contextualize their projects* to address the identities and needs of their unique students.
- *Plan and discuss implementation strategies* that allow for appropriate scaffolding and support.
- *Provide one another with feedback* on project quality, effectiveness of PBL teaching practices, and the student work that is emerging from the projects.
- *Develop a common and vested interest in the success of all students,* not just those in their own classroom.

Such collaboration may be new to some teachers. Ensure the availability of safe spaces and foster positive interdependence within and across teaching teams. Use staff meetings to model collaboration and shared responsibility practices you would like to see. Collaboration and shared responsibility are not one-time things; think about how to vary and deepen the practice over time. Here are some suggestions:

- *Co-create learning agreements for staff meetings* with your teachers using a process they can replicate with their grade-level teams and students.
- *Plan collaborative experiences* that also allow you to get to know your teachers. You want to understand their identities, hopes, dreams, and aspirations. How can you ensure each teacher feels that you and their colleagues see and value them for who they are and the gifts they bring?
- *Model discussion protocols and structures* that provide safe spaces and equity of voice for teachers to give one another feedback on practice and the quality of the projects they are implementing. We love the thinking routines provided by Harvard's Project Zero (https://pz.harvard.edu/thinking-routines) and the 30 Minute Virtual Tuning Protocol provided by the Center for Leadership and Educational Equity (https://www.clee.org/resources/30-minute-virtual-tuning-protocol/).
- *Ask teachers for feedback* on your work and make it a habit to thank them. You'll be surprised how many will start to come to you in turn. Be sure to model kind, specific, and helpful feedback.

Making Work Visible

One of the best ways to celebrate and improve on PBL—and, we believe, a must-have for any PBL school—is to make student work visible by sharing schoolwide and with the community at large. To that end, student presentations of learning should be regular events embedded in school culture. Whether in the form of student learning posted on the walls, a class project showcase, a whole-school exhibition with community members and experts invited, or more formal presentations of learning, making work visible has multiple benefits. Students, teachers, and leaders are almost always more inspired to do their best when they are creating work for an authentic audience. Students often say things like "I was nervous, but I'm so proud of myself for doing this," "I loved sharing and learned so much from what others shared," or "I didn't realize how much I learned until I was sharing it with others." Preparing work to share with others involves high levels of self-reflection, metacognition, and a deeper understanding of content—it helps to make learning more "sticky." Making students' work visible produces a sense of pride, ownership, responsibility, and engagement from students, teachers, and leaders.

Some teachers and leaders may be reticent to increase visibility for student work because it requires high levels of vulnerability, and to be frank, it's often an extra demand on teacher preparation time and energy as well as classroom time. But in our work with teachers, schools, and districts, we have repeatedly heard from students, teachers, and leaders that the time invested was well worth it. The sense of accomplishment, the opportunity to share who they are and how they have changed as a result of their project work with others, and the chance to be an "expert" and to be celebrated for it stay in the hearts of students, teachers, and leaders long after the event. Community pride, transparency, and involvement also grow in schools that regularly make their work visible.

Here are some suggestions for making work more visible in your school:

- *Encourage teachers to display visual artifacts of PBL,* such as project walls, throughout their classrooms.
- *Cultivate community partnerships* to support projects, allowing community members to authentically engage with students and support the school.

- *Replace a regular staff meeting* with a teacher-driven exhibition where individuals or teacher teams share their projects with others. They can share the driving question, project learning goals, process, sample student work, and reflection and lessons learned.
- *Host a grade-level (or schoolwide) project exhibition* at the end of the semester and ask each class to exhibit their project work. Invite families, community project partners, and other stakeholders.

Celebrating Success

As a PBL leader, you should regularly recognize and celebrate teachers and students for achieving deeper learning outcomes, especially through work that advances student equity. At the beginning of your schoolwide PBL implementation, you may not immediately see an impact on traditional student outcome indicators. Instead, you should look for uncommon indicators—ones that provide evidence that PBL is taking hold and going well. You might get an email from a parent saying their child has never been more excited about school or overhear a teacher sharing that using a PBL approach to teach the *Romeo and Juliet* unit resulted in more engagement and better essays than she has seen in her 20 years of teaching. You might notice a student who was formerly reluctant to engage in school come alive sharing his masterful graffiti art as part of a project exploring how street art can be a lever for social justice.

As we all know, both positive and negative energy can be contagious. Be sure to address the concerns and challenges beneath any negative energy with true empathy and compassion. At the same time, celebrate and lift up positive stories of success and impact to build momentum and excitement for PBL and inspire others to try it. Chip Heath and Dan Heath describe this approach in *Switch: How to Change Things When Change Is Hard* (2010). Rather than focusing on what is not working (which most of us are really good at), focus on what is working and why. Amplifying "bright spots" related to PBL makes practices more visible so that others can see what PBL looks and feels like, and you can get a better sense of how the implementation is going from different perspectives. It will also help you change hearts, which in our experience is a necessary precursor to changing minds. Suggestions for celebrating success as a leader:

- *Visit classrooms regularly* and share kind, specific, helpful, warm feedback to celebrate what teachers are doing well.
- *Share artifacts and stories* showing the impacts of PBL on student learning in your regular communications with staff and families. For example, add a PBL Spotlight Corner as a regular feature to your monthly newsletter.
- *Invite students to staff meetings* to share their project experiences and work. We have found that most students, from kindergartners to seniors, appreciate the chance to share their stories with their teachers.

Five Elements Intertwined

We hope you now have a better understanding of how you can build or strengthen the PBL culture in your context and that you are also starting to make connections between building a culture that supports PBL and deploying equity levers, especially knowledge of students and shared power.

As we learned in Chapter 1 from the discussion of equity and holonomy and symmetry, you should create and model for teachers the experience you want students to have. If you want students to demonstrate agency, you need to consider how you will give your teachers more agency.

The five elements of culture are intertwined. Focusing on even one of the five elements and its associated leadership practice helps harness energy to build and maintain a supportive culture that allows PBL to grow organically. If you start by making moves to foster more risk-taking, trust, and growth, people will feel inspired to make their work visible and celebrate success. If you start making work visible, student agency, collaboration, and shared responsibility are likely to increase.

Let's turn to a case study to learn how one leader built a culture for PBL in their school by focusing on making work visible.

Leadership Story: Making Work Visible

In 2019, Antonio Rael became the principal of Western High School, an urban school in central Las Vegas, Nevada, serving more than 2,700 students. His primary goal was to make learning more relevant and ensure Western was a beacon of pride for the students, staff, and community. He knew he needed to focus on pedagogy and culture to bring his vision to life, so he targeted the schoolwide adoption of PBL as a way to help teachers craft deeper, more meaningful learning experiences. Additionally, he emphasized celebrating the process, making both teacher and student work public and connecting student learning to the community.

To start the process, Principal Rael formed an elite team of campus-based stakeholders to act as catalysts for change. This team included two teachers who were early adopters of PBL, Mrs. Butanda and Mr. Rosero, whose enthusiasm for PBL and strong commitments to Western's students and families made them ideal for a grassroots movement. Principal Rael also identified Assistant Principal Mrs. de Young as the person to lead the instructional transformation necessary for PBL to thrive; her steady contributions would prove essential to the structured success of the PBL work. Alongside PBL, Principal Rael prioritized which initiatives would have the strongest impact on student and staff culture, community relationships, and academic achievement. To accomplish these goals, Principal Rael grew the career and technical education program, instituted a work-based learning program, and fueled the development of an excellent fine arts program. His emphasis on building each of these programs meant that Western could cultivate relationships with community members who could then play integral roles in future school projects.

Significant school improvement can be difficult, laborious, and inconsistent. It can often feel like everything needs to change all at once. The pressure to transform seemingly overnight can be overwhelming. Principal Rael, however, knew that forcing drastic change wouldn't win over the hearts and minds of the teachers, students, or community. Instead, he trusted the process and the team he'd empowered to do the work over time. Knowing that the success of PBL implementation would hinge on his ability to motivate and excite teachers, he opted for a gradual adoption of PBL across core content areas. Not every teacher was expected to leap into PBL at the same time. Instead, Principal Rael and the PBL Leadership Team sought to encourage teachers' curiosity about PBL and what it might look, feel, and sound like in their classrooms. They intentionally removed implementation barriers by ensuring teachers had access to PBLWorks workshops and routinely shared new learning across departments and grade levels.

These initiatives led to Western hosting a one-day project experience for every teacher on campus called Project Slice. Teachers took on the role of students and engaged in a project together to better understand how their students might experience PBL. Working through a project experience themselves started important conversations among the teachers about what PBL is and how it differs from traditional group projects. It also helped the school cultivate a campus culture of risk-taking and sharing work in progress.

A notable result of Western's engagement in the PBL Leadership Series workshops was a commitment to making teacher and student work visible during the 2023–24 school year. Principal Rael dedicated at least 20 minutes during each staff development day to a PBL Showcase, in which teachers shared their projects with the whole staff, including what products students were creating, the driving questions students were pursuing, and how various project ideas connected to specific PBL design elements. What made these PBL Showcases even more powerful was the addition of students' stories. Alongside their teachers, students shared what they were learning, how they were learning, and what made PBL different from their past experiences. They communicated how they felt more engaged and motivated by their authentic work and how powerful it was for them to connect to the world beyond the classroom. Each showcase was followed by monthly professional development sessions spearheaded by Mrs. de Young on specifically chosen PBL design elements to help teachers integrate these elements into every unit.

The PBL Leadership Team knew that if they wanted teachers to continue exploring PBL and implementing it in their classrooms, they would need collaborative and professional development time to appropriately prepare and tailor classroom instruction. Having ample time to prepare and reflect on project implementation resulted in substantial growth in teachers' confidence, and they started to open their doors during PBL for informal peer walkthroughs. Teachers became noticeably more comfortable allowing their projects' "messy middle" to be visible to their colleagues and leadership team. Consequently, as PBL work continues at Western, more stakeholders from caregivers to community members to content experts get to be a part of the incredible learning happening on campus.

Culture-Building Practice

To help you put your new knowledge into practice, use the following mini-trials to explore what it's like to build a culture for PBL. We encourage you to try at least one thing from either list. Afterward, record your reflections and note any new insights you acquired.

Individual Actions

- Visit another school's PBL exhibition or presentations of learning to gain inspiration for your school or district.
- Spend a day shadowing a student to understand your school's current reality related to PBL culture. Engage in everything your student does and pay close attention to how the student (and you!) experiences agency, risk-taking, trust, and collaboration throughout the day. How close is the "here and now" of what students are experiencing to your aspirations for "there and later"?
- Invite a teacher already using PBL to share project experiences, challenges, and successes with you. Ask what they think is needed to grow PBL in your school.
- Reflect on the set of questions in Figure 4.2 about the teacher culture in your school. How do you think your teachers would answer these questions?

Figure 4.2 Questions About Teaching Culture

1. Whom do you go to when you need support with a teaching challenge?
2. How would you describe the level of trust among your colleagues?
3. To what extent do you feel supported in taking risks or trying new things in your classroom?
4. How would you describe the amount of time allocated for and quality of collaboration between you and your peers?
5. How readily do teachers share their work and practice with each other?
6. To what extent do teachers influence or make decisions about how they use their professional learning time?
7. How often do you discuss problems of practice with other teachers in a structured format?
8. To what extent are the principles of Gold Standard PBL reflected in professional learning communities or professional learning experiences in your school?

Collaborative Actions

- At your next staff meeting, engage in a team-building challenge. The challenge should be easy to organize, require teamwork and communication, and initially be difficult for groups. You will show your teachers you believe in them by encouraging and supporting their productive struggle and ensuing success.
- Open your next small team or staff meeting with the Learning Circles activity detailed in Figure 4.3. Debrief the process with participants, asking them how it felt. Make a safe space to share joy, discomfort, and other emotions or offerings that might arise.
- Invite a teacher already using PBL to share their project experiences, challenges, and successes with other staff members. Follow up with a reflective discussion in which teachers share insights gained, how their current practice compares, and what support they would need to implement PBL in their classrooms.
- Discuss the questions about teacher culture found in Figure 4.2 with your leadership team or teachers.

Figure 4.3 PBLWorks Learning Circles Activity

Learning Circles

Providing the space for connection is at the heart of why we advocate for using a Learning Circle structure. Through this process, we build a community of PBL practitioners.

In Learning Circles, participants network to build relationships with others doing the same work they are so that reciprocal learning and support can exist beyond and outside the workshop.

Regardless of age or background, we can all better focus on new learning after being invited to share and acknowledge ourselves and those we are learning alongside. We set the stage by establishing groups of four to six people that stay together across an extended period to build trust and authenticity.

During each gathering, we repeat this process:

1. Share a moment of quiet for Learning Circle members to check in with themselves.
2. Read aloud or share an inspirational article, poem, quote, or video.
3. Spend time on open journal writing to put thoughts to paper. (Sharing is completely optional.)
4. Give each Learning Circle member a few minutes* to share whatever is on their mind.

*The heart of Learning Circles is holding space for each person to experience constructivist listening. This means we each take two minutes to "check in." You can share anything you want, or you can choose to be quiet. But it is your two minutes. There is no cross talk. Once everyone has their sacred time, the group is encouraged to have a more open discussion.

Copyright © 2016 Buck Institute for Education. Reprinted with permission.

Reflect

What did you try? What did you learn from your experience?

How has your view of your role as a culture leader shifted?

What are one to three concrete steps you can take for quick wins to build the culture you desire and need to advance PBL successfully in your context?

REFLECT

Final Reflections

1. Look back at your original mental model of school culture. How does it connect to what you just read about building a culture to support PBL? Did your thinking change? If so, in what ways? If not, why not?
2. What specific aspects of your current school culture align with the elements of PBL culture? How might you nurture these aspects?
3. PBL culture leaders naturally foster student agency; a culture of risk-taking, trust, and growth; collaboration and shared responsibility; visible work; and celebration of success. Who are your culture leaders on campus? What can you learn from them? How might you elevate their practices in a way that inspires others?
4. Go back to the leadership story featuring Western High School. In what ways did Principal Rael build a culture for PBL? How could you apply those actions to your setting or practice?

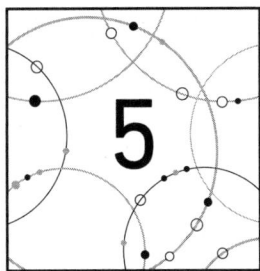

Designing the Infrastructure

How you spend your time is how you enact your values.

—Buffy Cushman-Patz, founder and executive director, SEEQS: The School for Examining Essential Questions of Sustainability

When Bob began his tenure at PBLWorks in 2015, he spent time in the field listening to teachers and educational leaders about their desire to implement project based learning. He learned that the teachers loved our three-day professional development workshops and came away excited to make PBL happen in their classrooms. However, they reported, more often than not, "doing school" got in the way of actually facilitating a PBL unit with their students. They didn't have enough time to finish planning or prepare for the project and were hungry for their instructional coaches and school leaders to provide additional support.

At the same time, school leaders often shared that they did not know what role they should play in PBL implementation because the workshops focused on teachers. One superintendent said, "We paid for all of our teachers to do your three-day workshop, and I told them they were expected to design and facilitate at least two projects. When I visit our schools, I don't see many teachers doing projects with students." One of the most important things a PBL leader can do is create the infrastructure that supports teachers in implementing PBL. They can further support their staff with this work by integrating capacity building into teachers' daily work.

In this chapter, we explore what we mean by infrastructure so you can better plan how to put conditions in place to enable teachers to do great projects with their students. These conditions can be considered within the four domains of our Logic Model (Figure 1.6): vision, culture, capacity building, and continuous improvement.

> **Reflect**
> **What does your current mental model of school infrastructure look like? Feel like? Sound like?**

Vision

As we discussed in Chapter 3, it is critical that you, as the leader, identify the "why" behind PBL implementation. It is equally important that you share your organization's vision and "why" across the community with parents, students, teachers, and staff. Sharing a vision statement, possibly accompanied by a graduate profile, sets the organization's North Star for this work. Effective PBL leaders create a comprehensive communication plan to share these collective values succinctly, early, and often in the rollout of PBL.

Culture

As you learned in Chapter 4, a PBL culture requires time for teachers to collaborate, time for students to engage in deeper learning, and time for both teachers and students to make work visible. The traditional school schedule comprising 45- to 60-minute lesson periods for each subject will present an obstacle for most projects. Leaders need to work to develop master schedules (or interim schedules during PBL implementation) that allow for longer blocks of time for students to work on projects, conduct field studies during the knowledge-building project phase, and present their learning to authentic audiences and for teachers to collaborate, prepare instruction, and assess deeper student work.

As outlined in Chapter 4, PBL leaders must commit to creating a culture of persistent learning and positive risk-taking. Although learning new skills can be intimidating for teachers who never want to fail their students, as a leader, you must foster an environment in which teachers feel supported to implement PBL even when they don't feel completely comfortable with it. Like students, many teachers learn by doing. Effective PBL leaders model the process by being vulnerable and taking risks when facilitating adult learning and regularly sharing their learning with staff.

Capacity Building

Capacity building begins when teachers attend a PBL workshop and continues through ongoing learning opportunities at the building level. Not only do teachers need time to share wins and collaborate on how to address implementation challenges, but they also need teacher leaders (e.g., grade-level leads, department heads) to be prepared to facilitate their PBL learning. As a leader, you need to consider the following questions:

- How might you model PBL practices during building-based professional learning? Who is equipped to help you plan and lead? Will you design inviting professional learning and model what high-quality PBL looks like?
- How will you inspire teachers and invite them into the work?
- How will you ensure teachers have adequate training and support to do PBL well?
- How will you ensure they don't get overwhelmed?

Leaders must also prioritize allocating time and staffing resources to support PBL coaching for teachers and redesign hiring practices to recruit and retain teachers with a desire to implement (and, ideally, experience with) high-quality PBL. Develop a consistent approach to sourcing and selecting teachers and staff who can facilitate and support PBL instruction, including creating a hiring pipeline for leaders and teachers that prioritizes PBL experience and commitment.

Continuous Improvement

As you move toward all students, especially marginalized students, experiencing high-quality PBL, identify the evidence you will use to evaluate your progress. As you consider the infrastructure required to sustain high-quality PBL, one of your first steps should be to determine what tools and processes your school will use to monitor the actual implementation of PBL (i.e., did teachers facilitate a project or not, and if so, with whom?). Next, address how your teachers and school will record and analyze student learning results based on their projects, products, and reflections on learning. Finally, to collect what Shane Safir refers to as "street data" (Safir, 2017), make plans for regular school-level presentations of learning to assess and refine implementation.

To support this work, we have created a School Conditions Inventory (Figure 5.1) to help you better understand your current reality across all four domains of our logic model and to help you identify high-impact action steps. We invite you to pause to review the inventory and assess where your school currently falls on the continuum.

> **Reflect**
>
> **Consider how well your school's infrastructure meets the conditions to support PBL. Where are you well prepared for success? What areas are there for growth?**

Figure 5.1 School Conditions Inventory

Use this inventory to assess the infrastructure and other school conditions necessary to implement Gold Standard PBL effectively.

Dimension: Vision	Continuum			
Condition	1 Not True	2 More Untrue Than True	3 More True Than Untrue	4 True
The district's graduate profile has been adapted to be specific to our school and is visible in our school's vision, mission, and school plan.				
Our school's vision statement elevates PBL as the primary instructional method to achieve deeper learning outcomes for all students, including those who are furthest from opportunity; this vision statement drives our instructional and operational decisions.				
Our school's communication plan includes key messages about Gold Standard PBL, especially how it fits with other initiatives we are implementing.				
Student success at our school is defined as achieving deeper learning outcomes.				
Dimension: Culture	**Continuum**			
Condition	1 Not True	2 More Untrue Than True	3 More True Than Untrue	4 True
Our master schedule has been redesigned or adapted to ensure that all students have blocks of time for engagement in Gold Standard PBL so that they experience at least two high-quality projects each year.				
All students present their learning to the community at least twice a year.				
All teachers and all school leaders (including me) present their professional learning at least once a year.				

(continued)

Figure 5.1 School Conditions Inventory (*continued*)

Dimension: Capacity Building	Continuum			
Condition	**1** **Not True**	**2** **More Untrue Than True**	**3** **More True Than Untrue**	**4** **True**
Time: Our master schedule has been redesigned or adapted to ensure designated time for collaborative teacher planning focused on Gold Standard PBL.				
Adult Learning: Our school's professional development plan comprehensively and seamlessly integrates professional learning focused on Gold Standard PBL.				
Resource Allocation: Our school facility has sufficient spaces conducive to student project work and learning presentations.				
Adult Learning: Teachers have had time to design projects and learn Gold Standard PBL teaching practices effectively.				
Resource Allocation: In our budget, we have dedicated adequate resources for teacher coaching and other teacher support for implementing Gold Standard PBL.				
Our hiring tools (e.g., job descriptions, sample lessons) have been updated to reflect Gold Standard PBL teaching practices.				
Dimension: Continuous Improvement	**Continuum**			
Condition	**1** **Not True**	**2** **More Untrue Than True**	**3** **More True Than Untrue**	**4** **True**
We have the necessary technology to support the collection and analysis of data related to the implementation of Gold Standard PBL.				
We have established systems for timely data collection, progress monitoring, analysis of implementation, and deeper learning outcomes.				
We implement school-level presentations of teacher and leader learning to document our progress in implementing Gold Standard PBL.				

Copyright © 2023 Buck Institute for Education. Reprinted with permission.

Critical Levers for Infrastructure

Leaders are uniquely positioned to influence three key infrastructure components to support the growth of PBL: time, adult learning structures, and resource allocation. Figure 5.2 identifies leadership goals associated with these components.

Rethinking Time: The Master Schedule

School leaders usually learn the hard way that scheduling practices can have unintended consequences. For example, honors or advanced courses in middle or high school schedules can become a de facto tracking mechanism for a particular demographic. A PBL leader with an equity mindset examines the impact of their schedule on the allocation of time, personnel, and physical space throughout the day, week, and school year. Consider the following questions as you engage in this review:

- *Time:* Do *all* students and teachers have access to and enough time to engage in high-quality PBL?
- *Personnel:* Is at least one teacher on each team experienced with or trained in high-quality PBL?
- *Physical space:* Are community spaces available throughout the day for project work that takes students outside the classroom?

It is critical that leaders ensure that the master schedule does not exclude any group of students—especially those who have been historically underserved—from experiencing deeper learning through PBL. We encourage leadership teams to conduct a deeper learning equity check on their current schedule before implementing changes. Likewise, ensure that time allocation and course loads for teachers allow them to collaborate, plan, build their capacity, and assess student work.

Your master schedule can be an enormous resource or a troublesome hindrance to PBL implementation. The following conditions are necessary to ensure that all students can benefit from deeper learning:

- *Equitable access* to high-quality PBL, with no students excluded.
- *Large blocks of time* designated for students to work on projects both alone and in groups.
- *Flexible blocks of time* that students can take advantage of to expand and contract their focus as projects intensify and wane.
- *Scheduled time* in and outside of the school day for public presentations of learning.

Figure 5.2 PBL Infrastructure: Components and Leadership Goals

Infrastructure Component	Leadership Goal
Time	Our master schedule has been redesigned or adapted to ensure that all students have blocks of time for Gold Standard PBL so that they engage in at least two high-quality projects during the school year.
Time	Our master schedule has been redesigned or adapted to designate time for collaborative teacher planning focused on Gold Standard PBL.
Adult learning	Teachers have ample opportunity to learn and practice the Gold Standard PBL teaching practices.
Adult learning	Our school's professional development plan comprehensively and seamlessly integrates professional learning focused on Gold Standard PBL.
Resource allocation	Our school facility has sufficient space to accommodate student project work and learning presentations.
Resource allocation	Our budget provides adequate resources for teacher coaching and other teacher support for implementing Gold Standard PBL.
What infrastructure or conditions are in place at your school to support PBL? What conditions might you need to put in place?	

Copyright © 2018 Buck Institute for Education. Reprinted with permission.

Let's look at two examples of master schedules that are conducive to schoolwide implementation of high-quality PBL. As you review them, consider how some or all of these ideas could work in your setting.

Hillsdale High School, San Mateo, CA. Hillsdale High runs on a partial block schedule, with Periods 1–7 meeting on Monday for 47 minutes each. On Tuesdays and Thursdays, Periods 1, 3, 5, and 7 meet for 87 minutes; on Wednesdays and Fridays, Periods 2, 4, and 6 meet for 87 minutes. Advisory is offered four days a week, and an extended session called Tutorial takes place once a week for studying, tutoring, or one-on-one meetings with teachers or advisors. To graduate, students must demonstrate their academic knowledge and skills and reflect on their growth in a portfolio defense presentation, which younger students are invited to observe. The school calendar also embeds 10 hours of late start days throughout the year to allow seniors to meet with coaches to plan and carry out senior projects.

Katherine R. Smith Elementary School, San Jose, CA. At K. Smith School, every grade level (K–5) uses PBL as an instructional strategy, and they are explicit about how PBL helps prepare students for college. Projects are facilitated during periods designated as "PBL Time" and include literacy and content area learning goals. The school operates a traditional bell schedule from 8:00 a.m. to 2:00 p.m., with a 15- to 20-minute recess and a 30-minute lunch. Resource specialists support special needs students as much as possible in the students' classroom so that they stay connected to their project groups. Resource specialists participate in all of the school's professional development, ensuring their work connects seamlessly with grade-level PBL.

Rethinking Time: Collaborative Teacher Planning

Just as students need specific time set aside in their schedules for PBL to flourish, teachers need designated work time to improve their practice. Specifically, teachers need the following:

- Regular opportunities in the workday to learn about the Gold Standard PBL Essential Project Design Elements and Project Based Teaching Practices.

- Regular opportunities in the workday to collaborate on lesson design and monitor student progress.
- Time to observe one another and provide constructive critical feedback on project design and implementation.
- Time for teachers and school leaders (including you!) to present their professional learning at least once a year.

Some schools designate common teacher planning periods with grade-level or subject-area teams to facilitate collaboration. Some add non-student professional development days to the yearly calendar. And some schools allow teams to use budgeted funds for substitute teacher coverage, freeing up time to design projects, conduct peer classroom visits, use data to assess student needs to plan small-group instruction, and extend their learning through coaching opportunities.

While your school's schedule may differ significantly from the examples presented above, we have found that even small shifts can make a big difference. An easy first step is to review your current schedule keeping the conditions necessary for student and teacher success with PBL in mind. What do you have agency over? Where is time your friend? Where is it your foe? For example, time might be your friend if you can adapt existing grade-level professional learning communities (PLCs) to facilitate collaborative planning. It might be your foe if the teacher union requires a 66 percent vote of support from teachers to move to a block schedule. What small steps can you take to leverage time more effectively? Can you repurpose a staff meeting for teacher presentations of learning? Could an existing science fair structure be converted to presentations of learning for all students?

Rethinking Adult Learning Structures

Equally important to organizing time to support high-quality PBL for all of our students is thinking about how best to foster ongoing teacher learning about Gold Standard PBL. Learning new things takes practice as well as coaching and support. Many schools already have structures in place to support adult learning, such as grade-level or department teams, PLCs, staff meetings, or professional collaboration days. But often these approaches fall short of meeting teachers' learning needs. When we work with school and district leaders, we encourage them to examine their current practices to ensure they are moving from more traditional practices to ones that better support authentic adult learning. Figure 5.3 offers suggestions for rethinking your approach to adult learning structures.

The PBL Professional Learning Loop

Dedicating time for teachers to help one another refine their PBL practice is crucial for taking a project from the concept stage to deep, meaningful learning for students (Fester, 2022). Even when teachers start with fully designed projects, they need adequate time to situate and contextualize the project for their students. They also need time to discuss how project implementation is going and to monitor student progress. These conditions can often be met with grade-level PLC meetings.

Our PBL Professional Learning Loop (Figure 5.4) helps with this refinement process. The PBL Professional Learning Loop includes protocols to be conducted before (Tuning, Unit Unpacking Protocol), during (PBL Consultancy, Looking at Student Work Protocols), and after a project (Review with Rubric, Looking at Student Work Protocols) is implemented to help ensure equity of voice and a laser focus on the quality of project

Figure 5.3 Rethinking Adult Learning

Instead of ...	Try ...
Mostly sharing information and updates	Focusing on reflection and sharing celebrations and challenges
One-size-fits-all meetings	Voice and choice for participants to better meet them where they are
Conversations that lose focus or are dominated by a few voices	Using protocols to guide discussions and ensure equity of voice
Following an agenda with topics determined solely by leaders	Using an inquiry approach to design meetings based on teachers' current needs
Keeping teacher and student work private	Sharing teacher and student work through regular critique and revision

Copyright © 2019 Buck Institute for Education. Reprinted with permission.

Figure 5.4 The Professional Learning Loop

```
        Plan a
        Gold Standard
        PBL Project
   ↗                    ↘
Post-Project          Pre-Project
Protocols             Protocol
   ↑                     ↓
      PBL Professional
      Learning Loop
Conclude              Launch
the Project           the Project
   ↖                    ↙
        Mid-Cycle Protocols
```

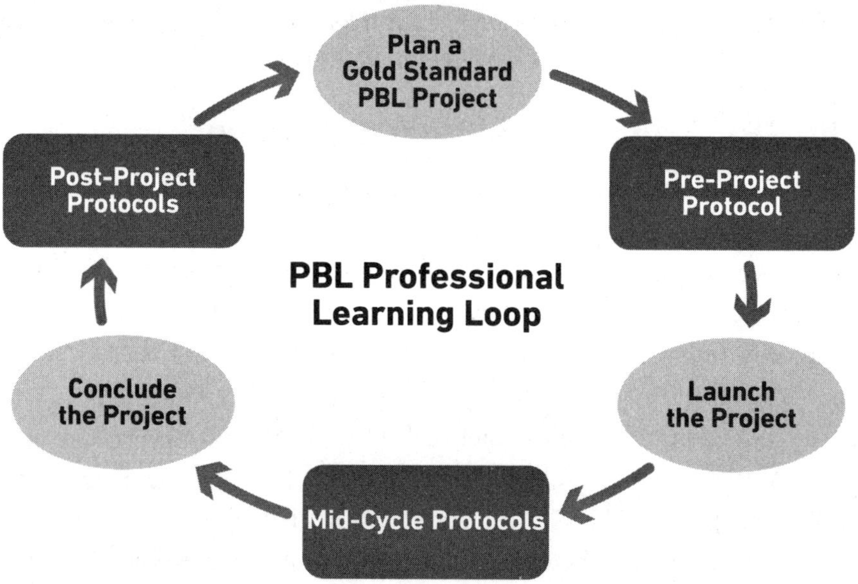

Copyright © 2019 Buck Institute for Education. Reprinted with permission.

implementation. It also models critique, revision, and reflection practices that can be used with students in a PBL classroom.

A more detailed guide to facilitating the PBL Professional Learning Loop can be found at https://bit.ly/PBLPLLG. Take a moment to think about how you might introduce or strengthen the use of protocols like these with your teachers.

The Professional Development Plan

It's common for teachers just starting their PBL journey to view projects as sequential events rather than a philosophy or core pedagogical approach to engage students with content meaningfully. In other words, they turn the PBL switch on and off, using PBL practices while working on a project and reverting to traditional instruction the rest of the time. Teachers who vacillate between approaches like this don't get enough practice with implementing the different aspects of Gold Standard PBL, leading to a weaker support structure for students when they engage in projects. National Faculty member Kristyn Kamps outlines this dilemma and provides a beautiful solution in her blog post: the "dimmer switch" approach. Kamps encourages teachers to try to use as many Gold Standard PBL Essential Project Design Elements as they can even in non-PBL unit plans. They can continue to "brighten" and use those elements, along with the Project Based Teaching Practices, to "keep the language and mindset of PBL alive" (Kamps, 2021, para. 17).

Successful PBL schools ensure their adult learning is laser-focused on developing teacher literacy in Gold Standard PBL and situated within a robust professional learning calendar that mirrors the Essential Project Design Elements and models the Project Based Teaching Practices. Ensuring teachers experience what Gold Standard PBL looks like and sounds like in staff meetings and other professional learning opportunities not only benefits the adult learners but also provides them with strategies they can use with their students.

Here are some suggestions for organizing your school's professional learning plan like a Gold Standard PBL project:

- *Start with a challenging problem or question* for the year, ensure clear learning goals, and identify how teachers will share what they have learned with others in relation to the learning goals.
- *Focus on one or two Essential Project Design Elements or Project Based Teaching Practices at a time.*
- *Model and use the language of Gold Standard PBL* in the design of staff meetings, PLCs, and any other professional learning or collaboration meetings to ensure teachers have a common language to discuss PBL progress and challenges.
- *Model the Project Based Teaching Practices,* such as co-creating learning agreements, balancing whole-group and individual learning options, using exit tickets as formative assessment, and using teacher questions to drive the agenda and learning for future meetings.
- Finally, *dedicate "sacred" time to discussing implementation wins and challenges* in staff meetings. Within this time, create the conditions for teachers to feel safe in sharing by taking an empathetic problem-solving approach, inviting teachers to share in advance, celebrating bright spots, and using protocols to discuss problems of practice. Once teachers experience success with PBL and receive authentic support with implementation bumps, they will be more likely to sustain the practice.

While you will learn more about how to bring adult learning to life in Chapter 6, you can take some small steps right away to ensure teachers have time to work on project design and implementation and that all adult learning integrates Gold Standard PBL. We suggest you revisit Figure 5.3 and consider acting on something from the "Try" column.

Rethinking Resource Allocation

The way we budget and allocate resources reflects our values. Leaders who prioritize students experiencing high-quality PBL must reinforce that value by ensuring their school, grade-level, and department-level budgets are sufficient to support teachers in their PBL implementation. Integral elements of PBL that are likely to require funding include the following:

- Field studies (transportation and possible fees)
- Guest speakers or expert consultants (travel costs)
- Project materials (e.g., technology, supplies, lab kits, printing)
- Exhibitions and presentations of learning (e.g., refreshments, off-campus venue rental, programs)

We often hear leaders lament that PBL is expensive to implement. Professional learning, transportation for field trips, materials, software, and technology may not fit easily into a decreasing school budget. But leaders driven to provide PBL to all of their students find a way to make it work. Some present each teacher with a prepaid debit card for their budgeted amount preloaded to give them agency in providing their students with what they need. Others leverage parents and community partners to support project implementation, either financially or materially. People often yearn for more meaningful ways to contribute to education beyond fundraising or organizing schoolwide events. Surveying families about their knowledge and expertise and inviting them to serve as content or industry experts, potential clients for a student project, or audience members for exhibitions is a strategic way to garner resources that don't rely on the school budget. Plus, in our experience, inviting the community and parents to participate in PBL often results in more engagement, enthusiasm, and financial support.

Rethinking Resource Allocation: Physical Spaces

Compared to traditional instruction, PBL often requires spaces that are larger or differently organized. Some schools are lucky enough to have the appropriate physical infrastructure, but the rest of us need to be creative to make space for collaborative student project work. Leaders need to ensure teachers feel empowered to reconfigure their classrooms. Ideally, the student furniture is movable so that teachers can thoughtfully arrange desks and chairs to encourage group work. If the desks cannot be moved, shared spaces like the cafeteria or multipurpose rooms can be scheduled equitably among teachers to use for project time. Arrangements also need to be made for presentations of learning to ensure there is sufficient space for both presenters and audience.

Some schools we work with have included students in the process of organizing physical spaces to support PBL. They identify an underutilized or overlooked space and make a project of reimagining the space with community members. Local builders, businesses, and community leaders are often interested in supporting such projects. You can even leverage high school or community college building and construction programs to serve as experts to help bring the idea to life. With a clear vision and an openness to thinking differently, most schools can find spaces to support PBL.

Rethinking Resource Allocation: Teacher Coaching and Support

We will explore building teachers' capacity in Chapter 6, including how to move beyond workshops to making a comprehensive and coherent plan for supporting teachers and sustaining the momentum after launching a new initiative like PBL. With this in mind, it is critical to realign resources like instructional coaches to specifically focus on facilitating high-quality PBL. Instructional coaches need to be trained in supporting the student-centered instructional activities inherent to effective PBL. Some schools we work with have converted instructional coaches into PBL coaches. Others have decided to make PBL the focus of all staff meetings, PLCs, and district-designated professional development days. Some engage in lower-cost book studies, create PBL resource hubs, encourage teachers to join free PBL webinars or professional learning networks, or partner with other schools to share professional learning costs.

As you rethink resource allocation, we encourage you to ensure that you center students who might not typically experience this type of deeper learning in your plan. Note ways you can redistribute your current school budget to support PBL for *all* students. Consider the following:

- What activities can be scaled back to free up time and resources for PBL?
- Are resources allocated in ways that allow all students to access PBL?
- Are there high-cost activities that could be adapted to fit within a project?

Now that we have fully explored rethinking time, rethinking adult learning, and rethinking resource allocation, let's turn to a case study to learn how one leader addressed the infrastructure challenge by rethinking time.

Leadership Story: Rethinking Time

Nestled in the middle of downtown Honolulu, Hawai'i, SEEQS: The School for Examining Essential Questions of Sustainability is a public charter school serving 180 middle schoolers in grades 6–8. Founded by Buffy Cushman-Patz in 2012, SEEQS strives to create a seamless link between academic content and real-world application through PBL.

The power of community is palpable on the campus because the school prioritizes designating time to build and maintain it. From the organization's inception, teachers and leaders were intentional about leveraging time in a way that reflected their values. In addition to centering their vision that "SEEQers will be stewards of planet Earth and healthy, effective citizens of the world," they identified as essential the concepts of interdisciplinary learning, student voice, play, teacher collaboration, teacher autonomy, and teachers following their passions. Other critical values include the following:

- *Ensuring students and teachers have adequate time together* to be whole people in academic and non-academic environments.
- *Creating a self-contained school experience* such that schoolwork and planning happen only during the school day for both students and teachers.

- *Amplifying the essence of each discipline,* providing time for teachers to teach the subjects they love, and understanding that each discipline is valuable in its own right.
- *Applying content and transdisciplinary knowledge and skills to real-world situations and contexts* that enable real-world learning.

SEEQS leaders realized early on that the schedule would need to be carefully constructed to authentically manifest their values throughout the school day. They recognized that time was a lever they could use to help them bring their vision, mission, and values to life. Cushman-Patz believes that in schools, as in life, time is the commodity in shortest supply. Her mantra is "How you spend your time is how you enact your values." She repeats this mantra often, and while the weekly schedule (illustrated in Figure 5.5) has evolved over the past 12 years, several fundamental elements have anchored its design from the beginning:

- *Physical activity to start the day.* Each day begins with physical activity to stimulate the brain. Students may choose from several course offerings and commit to different activities on different days. Offerings are determined by the initiative and interest of students, community members, parents, and teachers and range from gardening to dancing hula to basketball and more.
- *Later start time.* Most adolescents experience a "sleep phase delay, which means a tendency toward later times for both falling asleep and waking up" (Wolfson & Carskadon, 1998). In recognition of students' sleep habits, SEEQS academic content does not begin until 9:20 on most days, after Physical Activity, and begins at 9:30 on Wednesdays.
- *Interdisciplinary Essential Question of Sustainability (EQS) blocks.* As a fundamental part of the SEEQS experience, all students participate in an interdisciplinary PBL course designed around examining an Essential Question of Sustainability. These courses meet four days a week in two-hour blocks, which may include student-directed project time, teacher-led tutorials, community outings, guest visits, and, for upper-grade students, formal internships.
- *Academic content delivered over longer blocks.* EQS blocks are two hours long to enable various instructional approaches, groupings, projects, and activities. Core academic courses are 70 minutes long, allowing

Figure 5.5 SEEQS Weekly Schedule

	MONDAY	TUESDAY	WEDNESDAY Late Start	THURSDAY	FRIDAY	
8:30–9:15 (45 min)	Advisory / Play	Physical Activity		Physical Activity	Advisory / Play	Community
9:20–10:30 (70 min)	Mathematical Applications	English Language Arts	Mathematical Applications [9:30–10:40 (70 min)]	English Language Arts	Mathematical Applications	
10:35–11:45 (70 min)	Artistic Expression	Science Explorations	Artistic Expression [10:45–11:55 (70 min)]	Science Explorations	Artistic Expression	Content Courses
11:45–12:15 (30 min)	Lunch	Lunch	Lunch [11:55–12:25 (30 min)]	Lunch	Lunch	
12:20–1:30 (70 min)	Historical Perspective	Elective	Advisory / Townhall / Assembly [12:30–1:45 (75 min)]	Elective	Historical Perspective	
1:35–3:30 (115 min)	Essential Question of Sustainability (EQS)	Essential Question of Sustainability (EQS)	Historical Perspective [1:50–3:00 (70 min)]	Essential Question of Sustainability (EQS)	Essential Question of Sustainability (EQS)	Project Based EQS Courses
			Early Release			

Source: SEEQS: The School for Examining Essential Questions of Sustainability, Honolulu, HI. Reprinted with permission.

sufficient time for scientific lab activities, in-depth explorations in humanities, intensive reading and writing work in English language arts (ELA), student collaboration in mathematics, and much more. ELA and math blocks also enable time for focused intervention for struggling students.
- *Assembly and advisory.* Advisors serve as counselors for both social-emotional and academic needs. The weekly assembly is for all-school gatherings and community building and may include arts performances, honors or awards, or Town Hall meetings; advisory groups will sit together for assemblies and may meet afterward to debrief or check in. Students convene with advisory groups on Mondays and Fridays for morning activities.

Admittedly, SEEQS did not have to overcome the hurdle of altering an already-established schedule to create conditions that support PBL. Although they could have adopted a typical school schedule, they instead worked to create a schedule that reflects their values. Under Cushman-Patz's leadership, the schedule has evolved in response to student and teacher feedback. For example, in previous years, all math and science classes took place during the same window, followed by English and social studies classes in the second window before lunch. Arts and EQS classes were after lunch, with collaborative teacher planning during the Arts block. This resulted in the Arts teachers feeling left out and unequal to the more academic subjects. In response, school leadership made the Arts teachers full-time staff (equivalent to other content teachers), shortened content blocks a little, and added an elective block.

Students can also advocate for changes. During Town Halls, students can bring up motions for changes they want to see (e.g., more passing time). They also share their voices and get community exposure at public product exhibitions twice a year, presenting to an authentic audience of people they don't know. In these exhibitions, every student demonstrates a deep understanding of the natural world due to their ongoing exposure to real challenges and the opportunities to develop real solutions. Students benefit from the large blocks of time in their schedule to work on projects alone and in groups as well as from the teachers' access to a generous amount of co-planning time. EQS teaching teams meet from 8:00 to 8:25 a.m. four days a week and for even longer on the late start Wednesday—resulting in several hours of collaborative planning time every week.

Rethinking time for students and teachers at SEEQS has resulted in equitable access to high-quality PBL for all students and regular opportunities in the workday for teachers to collaborate and reflect on project design and implementation. As a result, students feel a strong sense of connection and belonging and feel they can be their "whole selves" while at school.

Infrastructure-Building Practice

To help you put your new knowledge into practice, here are some mini-trials that you can use to explore what it's like to build a solid infrastructure for PBL. We encourage you to try at least one thing from either list. Afterward, record your reflections and note any new insights you acquired.

Individual Actions

- *Visit a PBL school* and ask critical questions about their schedule, resource allocation, and adult learning structures to understand your school's potential.
- *Take a tour of your campus* to look for any spaces that could be redesigned or rethought to support PBL. Are there any unused or "junk" rooms that could use attention? Once you find one, invite some teachers and students to help you reimagine it.
- Check with your district to see if your school can *apply for grants* (e.g., innovation, social-emotional learning, personalized learning, assessment) to support your PBL initiative.

Collaborative Actions

- If you need to change your schedule, *start conversations with individuals or small groups about what works* with the current master schedule and what could be improved. You could even poll staff and students. Then, compare a few schedules from PBL schools to yours. What would need to change to better support PBL?
- *Review the Professional Learning Loop* and select a protocol to try with a small group of teachers. Make sure to leave time for reflection. Debrief after the protocol by asking the participants what their biggest takeaway was, what worked, and what could have worked better during the protocol.

- *Review your budget* and look for opportunities to reallocate resources to support PBL. For example, can materials and supplies be repurposed for projects by asking teachers to share how they are used for projects?

> **Reflect**
>
> **What did you try? What did you learn from your experience?**
>
>
>
>
> **How has your view of your role in creating the conditions to support PBL shifted?**
>
>
>
>
> **What are one to three actions you can take for quick wins to strengthen the infrastructure to support your vision for PBL?**

REFLECT

Final Reflections

1. How is your mental model for infrastructure evolving? How are you thinking about time, adult learning, and resource allocation as they relate to creating the conditions for PBL to thrive in your school?
2. Refer back to the School Conditions Inventory. Where are your strengths? Where are your opportunities to grow?
3. How might you repurpose staff meetings and other professional learning days/times to support PBL? How could you rethink your communication of traditional updates to free up time in staff meetings?
4. What specific aspects of your current professional learning structures align with the elements of adult learning for PBL? How might you increase your focus on these aspects?
5. What line items in your budget can be repurposed to support PBL? For example, could you require teachers to show how a field trip connects to a project when they request funding?
6. Look back at the description of SEEQS. In what ways did the school's leadership create conditions for Gold Standard PBL to flourish? What elements could you apply in your setting or practice?

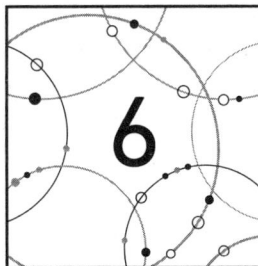

Building Capacity: Gold Standard PBL

We talk about "building capacity" as if teachers arrive empty, waiting to be filled. But teachers are among the most capable professionals we know—rich in expertise, creativity, and wisdom. Our job isn't to build them; it's to illuminate their strengths, elevate their practice, and create the conditions where their brilliance can be shared, refined, and multiplied.

— Dr. Krystal Diaz, Leading Heart and Mind & PBLWorks National Faculty

The greatest gifts you can give your teachers are to recognize their brilliance and to develop your own instructional eye for Gold Standard PBL so you can support teachers in developing theirs. Capacity building is developing skills related to the design, facilitation, and implementation of PBL—with the additional goal of being able to help build capacity in others. Every student deserves a teacher who can provide them with high-quality PBL experiences that include authenticity, collaboration, project management, reflection, public products, and intellectual challenge and accomplishment. At the same time, every teacher deserves a leader who can support them in improving their PBL planning and implementation. This requires a "leader as lead teacher" mindset and a commitment to cultivating ongoing opportunities for your teachers to expand and refine their PBL knowledge and practice.

KNOW

> **Reflect**
> **What is your current mental model of building capacity to lead a new initiative? What does it look like, sound like, or feel like?**

As we established earlier, leaders are key accelerators with a significant impact on student and school outcomes (Grissom et al., 2021). Building an ecosystem of support doesn't happen overnight, but the process is faster for leaders who prioritize developing capacity in themselves and their staff. Scaling up the implementation of PBL schoolwide requires that central adults in and around the school possess the necessary skills, knowledge, and mindsets to lead PBL—and this *must* go beyond teachers leading students to include the principal and other instructional leaders working with teachers. Although external high-quality professional development and training offer undeniable value, they alone are not sufficient. Consultants eventually leave, so what happens if your teachers need help the day after they are gone? Ensuring deeper learning and more equitable outcomes for students requires sustained effort and support, much of which should come from you and other school instructional leaders (Fester, 2022).

Instructional leaders make numerous decisions that can positively influence the successful implementation of PBL. One of your first decisions should be to commit to learning as much as possible about the approach. Building your capacity to recognize Gold Standard PBL in action will help you support teachers with implementing high-quality projects that advance learning for all students and accelerate learning for those most in need. You should set a goal of deeply understanding and becoming fluent in the Essential Project Design Elements and learning what Project Based Teaching Practices look, sound, and feel like in the classroom. In addition to developing your PBL instructional eye, you should work on designing and facilitating powerful adult learning experiences in staff meetings and

PLCs by leveraging protocols and routines that lead to productive PBL-focused conversations and teacher collaboration.

Figure 6.1 illustrates several critical elements of capacity building for Gold Standard PBL teaching and their associated leadership practices. We will address building capacity related to the assessment and grading of PBL in Chapter 7.

Figure 6.1 Capacity Building: Elements and Leadership Practices

Element	Leadership Practice
Gold Standard PBL: Essential Project Design Elements Rating: _____	I lead teachers in our school to regularly adopt, adapt, or design projects that include the Gold Standard PBL Essential Project Design Elements.
Gold Standard PBL: Project Based Teaching Practices Rating: _____	I have provided explicit guidance to teachers on adjusting the pace of the curriculum to ensure the regular use of Gold Standard PBL Project Based Teaching Practices that lead to deeper learning for students.
Professional learning: coaching and feedback Rating: _____	I ensure that teachers in our school have access to individualized coaching or feedback to support them in using Gold Standard PBL for deeper learning.
Professional learning: leadership development Rating: _____	I ensure that leadership team members and other teacher leaders in my school are engaged in formal professional learning opportunities or coaching to develop knowledge and skills to lead Gold Standard PBL for deeper learning based on their individual needs.

On a scale of 1 ("I have not yet explored this") to 4 ("This is central to my practice"), rate yourself on each leadership practice to evaluate your current reality and recognize where you need to focus your efforts.

After you've read the chapter, use the space below to reflect on what concrete steps you can take to build capacity in your faculty and staff to support PBL in your educational context.

Copyright © 2018 Buck Institute for Education. Reprinted with permission.

Gold Standard PBL: Essential Project Design Elements

We developed our research-informed model for PBL to help teachers, schools, and organizations improve, calibrate, and assess their practice. To lead teachers in your school to regularly adapt and implement projects that include the Essential Project Design Elements (see Figure 6.2), you must first know and be able to describe them. More importantly, you must learn to evaluate the quality of each element within a written project unit and be equipped to coach teachers toward higher-quality projects. In Gold Standard PBL, all projects focus on students acquiring key knowledge, understanding, and success skills—the learning goals at the center of the model. Each element contributes to students reaching these learning goals. Collectively, they describe and provide criteria for the design of a Gold Standard Project. Although the elements themselves are straightforward, designing an engaging project unit where each element is fully developed and aligned with all the rest is an art.

When supporting teachers practicing Gold Standard PBL, it is a good idea to begin by focusing on three components to ensure that the basis of the project is solid: Learning Goals, Challenging Problem or Question, and Public Product. Gold Standard PBL projects start with robust learning goals that include high impact or power standards and focus on at least one success skill. A good driving question needs to be open-ended (prompting multiple possible answers) and engaging. And students' public products should be authentic and allow them to share their answers and demonstrate mastery of the targeted learning goals and success skills.

Figure 6.3 on page 88 presents these three components pulled from PBLWorks's popular Making Space for Change project (https://my.pblworks.org/project/making-space-change). The driving question connects with students' sense of community and offers an open-ended challenge that they can approach on various levels. The final product and accompanying presentation will showcase students' critical thinking as they justify their decisions. Students' designs and explanations will provide evidence of the engineering principles and mathematical concepts they learned. And the presentation and subsequent audience questions will require students to practice their speaking and listening abilities. This is an example of a fully aligned project with a solid foundation.

Building Capacity: Gold Standard PBL 87

Figure 6.2 Gold Standard PBL: Seven Essential Project Design Elements

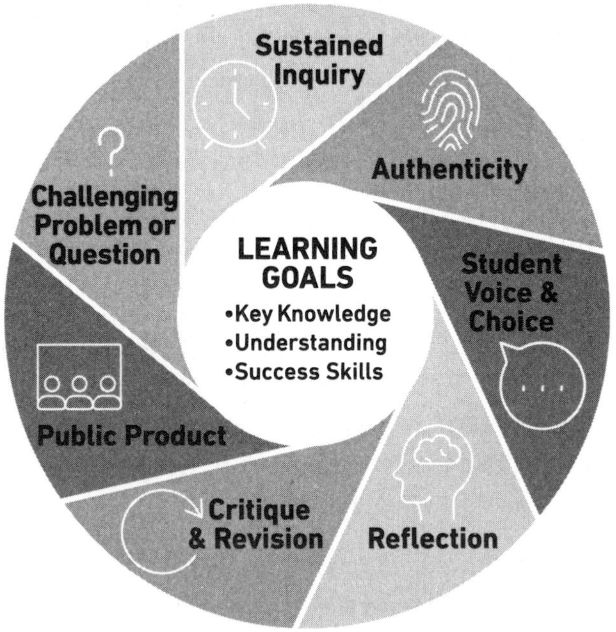

[Diagram: A circular pinwheel showing seven project design elements surrounding a central "LEARNING GOALS" with bullet points: Key Knowledge, Understanding, Success Skills. The seven elements around the circle are: Sustained Inquiry, Authenticity, Student Voice & Choice, Reflection, Critique & Revision, Public Product, Challenging Problem or Question.]

Challenging Problem or Question: The project is framed by a meaningful problem to be solved or a question to answer at the appropriate level of challenge.

Sustained Inquiry: Students engage in a rigorous, extended process of posing questions, finding resources, and applying information.

Authenticity: The project involves real-world context, tasks and tools, quality standards, or impact, or the project speaks to personal concerns, interests, and issues in the students' lives.

Student Voice and Choice: Students make some decisions about the project, including how they work and what they create, and express their own ideas in their own voice.

Reflection: Students and teachers reflect on the learning, the effectiveness of their inquiry and project activities, the quality of student work, obstacles that arise, and strategies for overcoming them.

Critique and Revision: Students give, receive, and apply feedback to improve their processes and products.

Public Product: Students make their project work public by sharing it with and explaining or presenting it to people beyond the classroom.

Graphic copyright © 2019 Buck Institute for Education. Reprinted with permission.

Figure 6.3 Making Space for Change

Challenging problem or question	How can we redesign a public space to promote a social benefit?
Learning goals	Develop critical thinking, engineering design, math, and speaking and listening skills.
Public product	Redesign a public space to promote a social benefit and present it to key stakeholders.

Copyright © 2023 Buck Institute for Education. Reprinted with permission.

Learning as much as possible about the Essential Project Design Elements will demonstrate to your teachers that you understand what they are working toward. As you build your capacity to lead teachers in your school to adapt and implement Gold Standard PBL projects, we also encourage you to do the following:

- *Participate in PBL training alongside your teachers* to create your own project. We have seen great success when leaders design a project with a driving question such as "How can I best support teachers in getting started with or deepening their PBL practice?"
- *Become familiar with PBLWorks's Project Design Rubric* (Appendix A) and refer to it regularly when working with teachers on project development. Many leaders we work with have copies of the rubric on their desks or displayed on a poster in the staff meeting room.
- *Review a few exemplar projects* and note how each design element is brought to life to get an idea of what good project design looks like. The myPBLWorks website (https://my.pblworks.org/projects) offers Gold Standard PBL blueprints and videos that you can use for this purpose.
- *Read Setting the Standard for Project Based Learning* (Larmer et al., 2015) to delve more deeply into what each design element can look like.

Gold Standard PBL: Project Based Teaching Practices

From our own experience as PBL teachers and our work with other teachers and leaders, we have learned that even a beautifully designed project that embodies all of the Essential Project Design Elements can go awry. This typically happens when a teacher is still becoming familiar with how to implement the Project Based Teaching Practices depicted in our model (see Figure 6.4). Becoming adept with these practices can help teachers address many common implementation challenges. Most teachers want a good first experience when trying something new and will be less likely to repeat the trial if they have a terrible experience. Thus, it is critical for leaders to know, understand, model, and provide support for the Project Based Teaching Practices every chance they get.

Many of these teaching practices will sound familiar to you because they are sound, effective, research-backed, and learner-centered practices teachers should be using already. However, bringing them to life in PBL often requires teachers to rethink their own role and identity in the classroom. Moving from being a dispenser of knowledge to a facilitator of learning can feel uncomfortable for teachers who thrive on tight instructional control. It can also be especially challenging for teachers who are having great success with their current practice or who have tried teaching with projects before with less-than-stellar results. We encourage you to meet teachers where they are and to celebrate any small wins along the way.

Regular and authentic use of the Project Based Teaching Practices can sometimes mean that teachers will need flexibility in their unit pacing. PBL emphasizes "uncoverage" over coverage. An uncoverage approach often requires more instructional time for learners to make deeper connections and engage in analysis and reflection. This is a good thing; it usually indicates that deeper learning is taking place. It also means that teachers often need more time to complete a topic or unit than is designated on their curriculum maps or pacing guides. Thus, it is important that you are able to provide the necessary latitude and permission to your teachers to adjust their pacing so they can fully implement the Project Based Teaching Practices.

As you work to get more comfortable leading your staff to regularly apply the Project Based Teaching Practices, we encourage you to do the following:

- *Participate in PBL training alongside your teachers* to observe how the facilitator models one or more practices and better understand what they look like in action.

Figure 6.4 Gold Standard PBL Project Based Teaching Practices

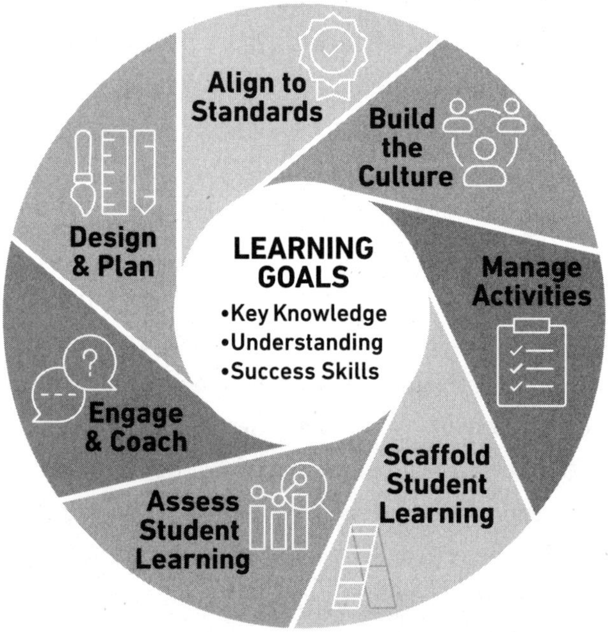

(Wheel diagram with center "LEARNING GOALS • Key Knowledge • Understanding • Success Skills" surrounded by: Align to Standards, Build the Culture, Manage Activities, Scaffold Student Learning, Assess Student Learning, Engage & Coach, Design & Plan)

Design and Plan: Teachers create or adapt a project for their context and students, and plan its implementation from launch to culmination while allowing for some degree of student voice and choice.

Align to Standards: Teachers use standards to plan the project and make sure it addresses key knowledge and understanding from subject areas to be included.

Build the Culture: Teachers explicitly and implicitly promote student independence and growth, open-ended inquiry, team spirit, and attention to quality.

Manage Activities: Teachers work with students to organize tasks and schedules, set checkpoints and deadlines, find and use resources, create products, and make them public.

Scaffold Student Learning: : Teachers employ a variety of lessons, tools, and instructional strategies to support all students in reaching project goals.

Assess Student Learning: Teachers use formative and summative assessments of knowledge, understanding, and success skills, including self- and peer assessments of team and individual work.

Engage and Coach: Teachers engage in learning and creating alongside students and identify when they need skill building, redirection, encouragement, and celebration.

Graphic copyright © 2019 Buck Institute for Education. Reprinted with permission.

- *Become familiar with our Project Based Teaching Practices Rubric* (Appendix B) and refer to it regularly when working with teachers to improve project implementation.
- *Watch PBLWorks's curated list* of Project Based Teaching Practice Videos at www.pblworks.org/gold-standard-pbl-teaching-practices-videos. Reflect on them and share with staff as appropriate.
- *Read Project Based Teaching* (Boss & Larmer, 2018) or one of the *Project Based Learning Handbooks,* available at www.pblworks.org/handbook.
- *Become familiar with and share the Strategy Guides* at https://my.pblworks.org/resources. Each unpacks key PBL instructional moves aligned to the Project Based Teaching Practices.
- *Model some of the practices in staff* or other collaborative meetings. For example, co-construct learning agreements with your teachers for staff meetings to build the culture. Or use exit tickets as formative assessments at the end of a meeting (assess student learning). Or provide different entry points or use a text-based protocol when introducing new material to teachers (scaffold student learning). The options are endless.

Professional Learning: Coaching and Feedback

The literature clearly states that to reform teacher practice in ways that will improve student outcomes, teachers need sustained, well-designed professional learning that focuses on content, pedagogy, or both. In a large-scale American Institutes for Research project that synthesized findings from more than 1,300 studies, researchers found that only professional development initiatives that included 30 or more professional development hours positively affected student outcomes (Yoon et al., 2007). Our learning in the field echoes these findings—sustaining PBL requires thoughtful, job-embedded, ongoing support. For some teachers, the shift to a PBL mindset and associated practices is seamless, and they require very little guidance. Others may need more reinforcement, and many fall somewhere in between. In other words, teachers need varied types of individual and group coaching even after the initial training. Although you may rely on external providers or experts initially, your goal should be to ensure that your own school community can eventually provide this support. To prepare for this stage, you need to consider how to offer ongoing PBL professional learning for all teachers while simultaneously building your capacity to provide individualized coaching and support. This will also allow you to recognize when others you designate to do this work are doing it well.

Keep the PBL Equity Levers in mind as you think about how to build your instructional eye for PBL to effectively support your teachers. Just as we want teachers to build knowledge of their students, as a leader, you should ensure that you acquire knowledge about your teachers. What are their interests, strengths, and identities? What do your teachers already know about PBL? Once you know this, you can better meet them where they are when designing and facilitating meaningful and engaging PBL professional learning experiences.

This work lends itself to a warm demander approach. This means ensuring an appropriate level of cognitive demand, rather than watering down the training or lowering expectations. Convey high expectations and the belief that every teacher can do PBL well, and provide appropriate scaffolds, supports, and tools to grow each teacher's PBL practice. Finally, consider how to share power with teachers in the process. How might you cultivate more teacher voice, choice, agency, and interdependence in service of teachers' ability to provide more agency to students? To build your capacity to offer individualized support, focus on two key practices: giving feedback and shifting from a consultant hat to a coaching hat when working with teachers.

Critique and revision are cornerstones of PBL, helping students and teachers get to what Ron Berger calls "beautiful work" (Gonser, 2021). To support teachers in incorporating these processes in a PBL context, leaders need to learn how to provide what Berger calls kind, specific, and helpful feedback (Berger et al., 2014). *Kind* feedback, delivered with empathy and compassion, is much more likely to be received well and acted upon. *Specific* feedback gives people precise direction on what to work on and helps them prioritize their actions in response. *Helpful* feedback is empowering—rather than just pointing out flaws, helpful feedback includes tools to accelerate growth, communicates that collaboration is valued, and builds confidence.

Many school leaders are expert consultants. They are used to offering solutions to teachers coming to them with issues, questions, or challenges. This dynamic works well for technical challenges or questions and is a necessary component of capacity building. However, supporting teachers with PBL often requires a more adaptive coaching approach. In coaching for PBL, the goal is to guide teachers to discover their own answers or solutions to their challenges. It involves asking great questions that inspire teachers to consider a different perspective using the lens of one of the teaching practices. Some simple yet effective coaching prompts include the following:

- How are you thinking about [essential project design element or teaching practice]?
- How did students respond to . . . ? Why do you think that was the case?
- What's working well in this project? Why?
- What are you struggling with? Why?
- Tell me more about how you . . . (e.g., established norms, taught students to collaborate, selected this driving question, are scaffolding key concepts).

Coaching PBL teachers in this way and offering kind, specific, and helpful feedback will build their self-confidence and help you uncover individual and shared needs that can inform professional development focus areas. Regardless of where they are on their PBL journey, all teachers need a safe space to share ideas, unpack challenges, and engage in dialogue that sparks new insight.

Here are some tips to take under advisement as you work to build your capacity to provide teachers in your school with appropriate coaching and feedback:

- It can take a while to become a PBL expert. *Give yourself grace* as you deepen your knowledge of Gold Standard PBL Essential Project Design Elements and Project Based Teaching Practices by focusing on a few elements or practices at a time.
- *Find ways to assess teachers' knowledge and implementation of PBL* to understand their coaching and feedback needs better. Our favorite way

is the "need to know" process, in which you ask teachers to brainstorm questions that come up for them, group and prioritize the questions, and then use them to design and develop tailored coaching and professional learning. Other means of assessment include formal or informal one-to-one conversations, classroom drop-ins, and regular PBL pulse surveys.

- *Take it slow.* Teachers don't have to jump into all the practices at once. For example, model and encourage using learning agreements, classroom routines, and protocols before diving fully into PBL.
- *Dedicate time for teachers to get individualized support* from a PBL expert early in the implementation process and participate in these efforts as often as possible so that you build your own confidence in the practice.
- *Ensure your schoolwide annual professional learning calendar centers one or two Essential Project Design Elements or Project Based Teaching Practices* each semester.
- *Consider holding a Teacher Presentation of Learning or Exhibition* in your first year of PBL implementation so teachers can share what they learned with each other.

Professional Learning: Leadership Development

By now, you have likely figured out that instructional leaders in a PBL school must be comfortable speaking the language of PBL, adept at providing guidance, and equipped with the skills and tools to lead PBL discussions and professional learning. Thus, it is critical that you provide a core group of instructional leaders with formal opportunities and coaching to develop their ability to lead for PBL.

Early in the implementation process, identify a group of instructional leaders (including teachers) who are fully committed to learning alongside your staff and, in the best-case scenario, to be a little ahead of the rest. This PBL leadership cadre or team should include representatives from various grade levels, subjects, and departments. It can consist of academic/instructional coaches, grade-level or department chairs, the librarian and technology coordinator, and others who provide academic support to teachers and students. It's also a good idea to include teachers with experience with PBL or opinion leaders who can provide insight on how staff might respond to the rollout. This group should determine the faculty's readiness to engage in PBL, suggest how best to roll out PBL across the school and community, provide teachers or students with support as appropriate to their role, and monitor implementation.

Your PBL leadership cadre should undergo formal PBL coaching or leadership training as well as standard PBL training for the most significant impact on leader practice. We structure our leadership support in districts using a community of practice (CoP) approach, which brings together leadership teams from different schools in a district or across districts to engage in full-day workshops over the course of 12 to 18 months. These workshops are complemented by strategically placed implementation calls and leadership learning walks. During implementation calls, principals reflect on progress and discuss wins and challenges to learn from each other. Leadership learning walks provide the opportunity for principals to visit each other's schools to see the work in action, address a specific problem of practice, and gain insight from one another. These structures allow leaders to learn, implement, reflect, and refine their PBL leadership practice in a safe and supportive space with other leaders doing the same work.

If a formal CoP structure is impractical or unavailable to you, there are many other ways to provide formal professional learning opportunities to your instructional leaders. These include PBL book studies, attending PBL conferences, taking online PBL courses, and reading and discussing articles and blogs written by leaders who have successfully implemented PBL. You may also want to consider the following:

- *Encourage your PBL leadership cadre to subscribe* to PBL newsletters, blogs, and podcasts and commit to spending one to two hours a week together discussing what you are learning.
- *Attend a PBL Coaching Workshop* (www.pblworks.org/services/pbl-coaching) with your instructional leaders to learn how to implement the PBL Coaching Cycle and build a PBL Coaching Toolkit.

- *Encourage your district to start a districtwide PBL coaching PLC* so that instructional coaches across schools can share ideas and best practices.
- *Engage in PBL-focused classroom walkthroughs* with different members of your PBL leadership cadre to learn more about teacher needs related to project design and implementation.
- *Partner with other leaders* in your district to consider how you might work together to provide resources for teachers and leaders to learn how to implement PBL.

Let's turn to a case study of how one leader built their capacity for Gold Standard PBL by focusing on the Essential Project Design Elements.

Leadership Story: Gold Standard PBL

Derrick Kellam, principal of University Preparatory Academy High School in Detroit, Michigan, looks at his watch and realizes it's time to head over to a session on project critique protocols that's about to take place with his 9th grade team. At a round table sit 9th and 10th grade teachers at University Prep, along with former and current students. In front of them are the Essential Project Design Elements rubric and copies of the project plans Ms. Hughes is presenting for feedback.

Ms. Hughes sets herself a five-minute timer and begins outlining the project's key learning standards, driving questions, and opportunities for student voice and choice. She explains the community interactions students will engage in throughout the process, how students will work together, what they will produce, and how they will be assessed during her project. The timer goes off, and Ms. Hughes's colleagues and students take a few minutes to gather their thoughts. They anchor their assessments in the rubric criteria and the PBL Equity Levers: knowledge of students, cognitive demand, literacy, and student agency.

In a round-robin, team members share feedback on areas of strength, key questions, and ideas to improve the project design. One student says, "My brother was in your class last year and loved this project. You did a great job bringing it back. My question for you is, how will you make it different for me this year?" There are nods from others around the table, likely because Ms. Hughes's colleagues often wrestle with the same question: How do they keep what they're doing fresh but not so new that the planning is overwhelming (again)?

At the end of the sharing protocol, the team invites Ms. Hughes to contribute her reflections on what she's heard and engage in a more open dialogue about the feedback and the improvements she might make for this year's 9th graders. She turns to the student who asked her the question and says, "You really have me thinking on this. It's challenging for teachers to keep things fresh but not feel like they are returning to the drawing board, because the planning process is intense. And I like this project. So did my students. The products were awesome, and the students performed well on the assessment. So I'm not sure. What ideas do you all have?" The conversation continues animatedly from there.

Mr. Kellam leaves the session feeling joyful at the authentic collaboration between teachers and students. It's uplifting to see how his work with the leadership team and teachers to pull the curtain back on the PBL design process has paid off. His vision is for students at the school, 99.3 percent of whom are students of color, to have the opportunity to see themselves in the learning they experience, and he is pleased that efforts to strengthen teachers' understanding of the characteristics necessary for truly Gold Standard PBL are resulting in exemplary projects.

When Mr. Kellam reaches his office, he pulls up Ms. Hughes's "scouting report," a running record of his evaluation of her strengths and opportunity areas, both observed and self-identified. He notes that Ms. Hughes is standing out as a leader in the project critique protocol process and reminds himself to ask her to share at the next faculty meeting how she is leveraging the power of student voice to improve her project design before implementation. He also notes that he should ask Ms. Hughes how she used her knowledge of this year's 9th grade class to contextualize her project. Finally, he reflects that, in addition to the round table being an opportunity for Mr. Kellam to see the protocol in action, it affirmed that Ms. Hughes is on track to implement her project at the time indicated on the project implementation chart that he and his administration team use to set support, observation, and coaching schedules.

Next, Mr. Kellam proceeds to Mr. McLaren's 12th grade English class, where students are working on a project to answer the question "How is identity shaped through place, interactions, and experiences?" As he goes, he reviews the notes he left himself on Mr. McLaren's scouting report to direct what he is looking for in this quick observation. He sees that making space for authentic student voices related to essential parts of the PBL process is a strength of Mr. McLaren's. For this pop-in, he decides to seek affirming evidence of that strength to add to his scouting report and share with Mr. McLaren. He'll also ask Mr. McLaren to discuss these strategies more broadly during a faculty meeting to reinforce the practice and build on it with both Mr. McLaren and others. "My goal is to support teachers in incrementally being consistent with the things they do well," he says. "I want to emphasize the strengths in my teachers so they do them all the time. Feedback on their areas of opportunity needs to be given in real time, with the expectation that teachers reflect and get concrete about what strategy they'll try to improve. And that's what I look for the next time. Slow and steady wins the race."

These snapshots demonstrate just two of the many ways Mr. Kellam has built his own capacity and the capacity of his staff and students to support Gold Standard PBL project development and facilitation. His emphasis on setting clear, high expectations and putting the systems and structures in place for teachers to meet them comes from acquiring a deep knowledge of his staff so that he can authentically coach, celebrate, and elevate them. Mr. Kellam's story also reflects how intentionally honoring student and staff voices can powerfully and positively influence a school's professional culture, leading him to trust that deeper learning for students through PBL will be a part of his leadership legacy.

Capacity Building for Gold Standard PBL in Practice

To help you put your new knowledge into practice, here are some mini-trials you can use to explore what it's like to build capacity for Gold Standard PBL. We encourage you to try at least one thing from either list. Afterward, record your reflections and note any new insights you acquired.

Individual Actions

1. *Evaluate a teacher project* using the Project Design Rubric (Appendix A). Identify the project's strengths and one or two design elements for improvement. If appropriate, find a way to give the teacher kind, specific, and helpful feedback.
2. *Review the agenda* for an upcoming staff or PLC meeting. How might you work with the organizers or presenters to model one to two Project Based Teaching Practices?
3. *Survey your teachers* to determine their interest in and experience with PBL. If your school has been implementing PBL for a while, ask about success, challenges, and support needs.

Collaborative Actions (Ideally with the PBL Leadership Cadre)

1. *Engage in a video analysis* of one Project Based Teaching Practice at www.pblworks.org/gold-standard-pbl-teaching-practices-videos. Start by having everyone review the Project Based Teaching Practices Rubric (Appendix B), watch the corresponding video together, and discuss. Focus on how your school's current reality for that practice aligns with the examples in the video. Identify steps to take to support teachers in better understanding and implementing the practice.
2. *Analyze one of the project videos* available at www.pblworks.org/gold-standard-pbl-videos. Start by having everyone review the Project Design Rubric (Appendix A), then watch the video together and discuss. Focus on things teachers at your school are already doing that align with what you see in the video and identify any gaps. Brainstorm and decide on steps to amplify bright spots to help close the gaps.
3. *Review the school's professional learning plan* for the year. Ask colleagues to individually determine the extent to which the plan centers Gold Standard PBL from a topic and process perspective. Invite the team to suggest ways to adjust the plan to better focus on one or two Essential Project Design Elements or Project Based Teaching Practices for an upcoming month, quarter, or semester.

Reflect

What did you try? What did you learn from your experience?

How has your view of your role as instructional leader of PBL shifted?

What are one to three actions you can take for quick wins to build the capacity you desire and need to advance PBL successfully in your school?

Final Reflections

1. Look back at your original mental model of capacity building. How does it connect to what you have read about capacity building for Gold Standard PBL? Did your mental model change? If so, in what ways? If not, why not?
2. Refer to Figure 6.1 and your initial self-assessment of your capacity building leadership practices. Using the same 1–4 rating scale, with 1 being "I have not yet explored this" and 4 being "This is central to my practice," how do you rate yourself after learning more about the practices? What are your strengths? Where are your opportunities to grow?
3. What are some specific aspects of your current reality that align with the elements of capacity building for Gold Standard PBL? How might you expand or improve on these?
4. Who are your PBL experts or leaders on campus? What can you learn from them? How might you lift their practices in a way that inspires others? If you can't identify any, who are your most promising PBL teachers? How can you build their capacity for Gold Standard PBL?
5. Revisit this chapter's leadership story. In what ways did Mr. Kellam build his capacity for Gold Standard PBL? What lessons could you apply in your own setting or practice?

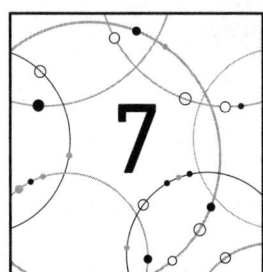

Building Capacity: Assessing Deeper Learning

Anytime you make the work public, set the bar high, and are transparent about the steps to make a high-quality product, kids will deliver.

—Ron Berger, author, *Leaders of Their Own Learning: Transforming Schools Through Student-Engaged Assessment*

Most educators, policymakers, and parents agree that today's students need a mix of knowledge, skills, and dispositions to prepare them to be successful and engaged citizens. But how do we know if students are learning both the content we are teaching and the skills they need to know to succeed? First, it's important to understand that the two domains are inextricably linked. Leaders focusing on deeper learning need to facilitate a process where schools and school systems clearly specify that students' graduate outcomes include not only courses or subjects passed but also deeper learning outcomes: mastering academic content, thinking critically, communicating effectively, collaborating productively, and learning to learn. In this way, we will create educational systems that ensure students are ready for success in college and career.

Once these outcomes are established, the next step is to create assessments to evaluate students' mastery of the outcomes. A simple multiple-choice test or grade based on assignment points will not suffice. Assessing deeper learning requires performance—for example, we assess students' collaboration skills by observing them working with their peers and reflecting on their interaction. In traditional instruction, assessment is often a top-down process done by teachers who decide where students are on the continuum of learning. In contrast, PBL engages students directly in assessing their own progress as part of the Know–Do–Reflect (KDR) approach to learning.

> **Reflect**
> **What is your current mental model of assessment and grading related to deeper learning?**

Assessment is also used to understand, inform, and improve teaching and learning. Although assessments may be graded, their primary purpose should be gathering information about student progress so the teacher and student can make targeted adjustments to support learning. Your role as a PBL leader is to help teachers shift from assessment *of* student learning to assessment *as, for, and of* student learning. In a PBL classroom, assessment should include strategic use of performance assessments and the following assessment practices:

- Project products and other sources of evidence are used to thoroughly assess subject-area standards and success skills.
- Individual student learning, not just team-created products, is adequately assessed.

- Formative assessment with a variety of tools and processes is used regularly and frequently.
- Structured protocols for critique and revision are followed regularly; students give and receive effective feedback to inform both instructional decisions and students' actions.
- Students are provided with regular, structured opportunities to self-assess their progress and, when appropriate, assess peers on their performance.
- Students and the teacher use standards-aligned rubrics throughout the project to guide both formative performance tasks and summative performance assessments.

In 2014, the Stanford Center for Opportunity Policy in Education (SCOPE) released a study (Friedlaender et al., 2014) that looked closely at four California high schools, including two of the schools Bob co-founded: Impact Academy of Arts & Technology in Hayward and City Arts & Technology High School in San Francisco. All four schools in the study serve predominantly low-income students and students of color. The study provided an "assessment of assessments" that shows what can happen in a PBL environment using the KDR framework. SCOPE's independent review of how students in deeper learning schools are succeeding in college offers compelling evidence in support of PBL:

- *College-ready coursework.* At two schools, City Arts & Tech and Impact Academy, 100 percent of Black and Latino 2012 graduates completed the courses required for University of California/California State University (UC/CSU) eligibility. Statewide, the rates are 29 and 28 percent, respectively. Additionally, 100 percent of low-income 2012 graduates completed the UC/CSU required coursework, compared to 30 percent statewide for both university systems.
- *College persistence.* Nationwide, only 8.3 percent of all low-income students earn a bachelor's degree by their mid-20s; at City Arts & Tech, where 73 percent of the student body is low-income, 72 percent of 2008 graduates and 85 percent of 2009 graduates persisted in college into their fourth and fifth years. The national college persistence rate for all incomes is 65 percent.
- *Standardized testing.* At Impact Academy in 2012, 70 percent of students scored proficient or above on the California Standardized Test for Algebra, compared to 36 percent statewide.

These results are attributed to students spending four years in classrooms that adhered to the three principles of the KDR framework:

- *Principle 1: Learn (Know).* Teachers design standards-aligned courses, lessons, and projects, ensuring students learn necessary knowledge and related skills through the deliberate integration of academic content, the arts, and career and technical courses.
- *Principle 2: Demonstrate (Do).* Students become experts at showing what they know through frequent PBL exhibitions and defenses of their work. This expectation translates to students having a more profound sense of connection to the content. They are motivated by an internal desire to learn rather than a desire to get a particular grade. One student described the sense of accomplishment that comes from demonstrating learning by explaining that it "pushes me a lot harder and makes me more proud of what I'm learning about. Especially when I can teach somebody else what I learned, it makes me feel better about learning that subject." Another described it like this: "Being put in a position to articulate a concept to an audience takes greater comprehension than just learning the idea for yourself. By talking about the project, I deepened my own knowledge of the math we were learning."
- *Principle 3: Reflect.* For each PBL unit and exhibition, students are asked questions such as the following:
  - What do you already know?
  - What have you learned along the way?
  - What do you still need to know or do to master the content?
  - How can you revise your work to make it stronger?
  - What have you learned about yourself in the process?

These questions help students internalize their learning and develop the growth mindset that leads to future college success and lifelong learning.

As the SCOPE research illustrates, students are transformed by the Know, Do, Reflect model integral to PBL. After high school, they are ready for college and better positioned for economic and personal success in their careers, communities, and society.

In addition to leveraging the KDR model, performance assessments, and other assessment practices of PBL, leaders must consider how to foster intrinsic motivation to work toward high performance in both teachers and students. Education is, of course, about so much more than filling minds with facts and figures. Teachers everywhere know that we are preparing students for various future experiences: college, careers that will evolve, and community and civic life. So how can we know if we are developing lifelong learners, active and critical thinkers, and informed citizens? One way is to ensure students have ownership and agency in the assessment process through critique and revision protocols anchored in well-designed rubrics that are aligned to learning goals. Another is to engage students in authentic performance assessments. The right kinds of assessment can inform us beyond whether students are gaining knowledge or not.

In Chapter 6, we unpacked the first four elements associated with capacity building related to Gold Standard PBL coaching and leadership development. This chapter homes in on the elements and leadership practices related to assessment and grading (see Figure 7.1). To begin the discussion, we present four key pillars of PBL assessment and grading.

- *Common performance frameworks and rubrics.* Use common frameworks and rubrics across grade levels and departments in the school and the school system so that educators can share tasks and calibrate the criteria so that mastery means the same thing systemwide. If every teacher and every school follow a different framework or rubric, it is impossible to come to a common understanding of the level of mastery as demonstrated in student outcomes.
- *Exemplars.* Teachers and school leaders need exposure to exemplars, including high-quality student work and ready-to-use deeper learning performance assessments to understand how PBL comes to life in instructional design and student work samples. Exemplars set expectations for quality and provide inspiration and guidance as teachers work to improve their practice.
- *Equity and access.* For students to show what they know and can do, assessments need to be learner-centered, asset-based, and accessible to all students. They should be embedded in meaningful contexts and leverage students' interests, experiences, and knowledge of their cultural identities and communities. To ensure all students are engaged, project assessments should use and allow for multiple

modalities, be developmentally appropriate, and provide varying degrees of scaffolding based on students' needs, particularly those of multilingual learners and special education students.

- *Time for capacity building.* As we discussed in Chapter 5, deeper learning requires us to rethink how we spend time during school days and professional learning. Teachers need time to learn about and assess PBL work. This requires focused, well-planned, leader-facilitated professional development and time at staff or department meetings allocated to assessment discussion.

Figure 7.1 Capacity Building: Elements and Leadership Practices for Assessment and Grading

Element	Leadership Practice
Assessment Rating: _____	I monitor and support the regular use of performance assessments that give students an opportunity to show what they know and can do throughout a project.
Grading Rating: _____	I monitor and support the regular use of standards-aligned rubrics as a grading practice for projects.

On a scale of 1 ("I have not yet explored this") to 4 ("This is central to my practice"), rate yourself on each leadership practice to help determine your readiness to lead capacity-building efforts for assessment and grading at your school and decide where to focus your efforts.

After you've read the chapter, use the space below to reflect on what concrete steps you can take related to PBL assessment and grading in your educational context.

Copyright © 2018 Buck Institute for Education. Reprinted with permission

Assessment

To monitor and support the regular use of performance assessments, leaders must first understand precisely what performance assessment in PBL should look like and how to identify it. According to Brown and Mednick (2012), high-quality performance assessments feature the following characteristics:

- They are engaging and meaningful for students.
- They measure real-world skills and knowledge.
- They include opportunities for students to receive feedback that motivates them to continue learning.
- They allow students to demonstrate mastery of the content and skills they have learned.

Applying the KDR framework to PBL enables us to view an entire project as a performance assessment. With each unit aligned to specific disciplinary standards and success skills and group and individual tasks running concurrently throughout the unit, the project is a single, complex performance assessment that provides opportunities for teaching and learning (know), student demonstration (do), and self-evaluation (reflect). Individual products can be viewed as embedded performance tasks. The final products should merge content with real-world applications in an authentic context. Authentic performance assessment measures content standards, disciplinary skills, and success skills such as communication, collaboration, critical thinking, self-directed learning, and creativity.

One way to assure yourself of the validity of a performance assessment is to consider whether preparing for the assessment, engaging in the assessment, and applying the skills in real life all look the same. Think of the most common real-world performance assessment: getting your driver's license. First, you demonstrate your knowledge of the rules of the road with a permit test—an essential step in the process, but not as important as demonstrating how you apply your knowledge in real life. That's where the performance or driving test comes in. Consider the specific skill of parallel parking (or any other driving competency). How do you learn and practice it? By parallel parking. How are you tested for this skill when getting a driver's license? By parallel parking. And what do you do with the skill after you pass the test? You parallel park.

In this light, the value of authentic performance assessment in school becomes more apparent. We can see exactly how vital "doing" is to the learning process, and we can agree that a driver's license should only be awarded to someone who knows not just the rules of the road but also how to operate a car to follow them. PBL asks students to practice and demonstrate command over the very skills they need for the next step in their learning journey. Sometimes, that next step happens tomorrow or next week, and sometimes it begins years down the road. Traditional assessments, even when they include open-ended questions or are performance-based, only give us part of the picture of a student's readiness for college and career success. Performance assessments prepare students to keep looking ahead for more learning opportunities to integrate with what they are currently investigating.

While getting started with PBL performance assessments might seem daunting, you can start to build your capacity to support teachers with assessment by engaging in one or more of the following activities:

- *Attend PBL exhibitions* and presentations of learning at nearby schools to better understand what good performance assessments look like and envision the possibilities for your school.
- *Learn as much as possible about quality performance assessments* from colleagues and other experts.
- *Connect the KDR framework with the use of performance assessments.* Once you understand how they connect, it will be easier for you to support teachers in realizing that increasing students' content knowledge alone isn't enough to prepare them for the future. Performance assessment requires knowing, doing, and reflecting throughout a project.
- *Become familiar with the types of authentic products* that serve as solid evidence of student learning from a project. These include debates, poetry slams, mock trials, plays, brochures, field guides, podcasts, videos, photo essays, social media campaigns, scale models, proposals, blueprints, and business plans. PBLWorks has developed a set of Product Toolkits (https://my.pblworks.org/resources) that can help teachers learn how to plan and scaffold products for each phase of PBL.
- *Gain an understanding of your current reality* by reviewing project or classroom assessments to determine the degree to which they align

with the characteristics of high-quality performance assessments described on page 108.
- *Give teachers explicit permission to use performance assessments* and encourage them to do so. Don't forget to provide them with adequate and sustained professional learning in this area.
- *Engage in the Professional Learning Loop protocols* (see p. 72) alongside your teachers to monitor and better understand the caliber and use of performance assessments in your school.

Grading

Traditional grading methods often do not align well with the goals of PBL. Grading in PBL should emphasize collaboration, process, and authentic learning. Teachers often grapple with questions about assessing individual student performance in group projects, balancing formative and summative assessments, and maintaining student motivation without relying solely on grades.

PBL leaders must make time to address teachers' grading challenges. We find the best place to start is with grade- and department-level leaders. Work with building and teacher leaders to establish a schoolwide grading policy and an assessment plan. Once you agree on your vision for assessment, it is essential that you share the plan with the entire staff for feedback to help build capacity in the area of assessment and grading as a community.

Key Strategies for Grading in PBL

John Larmer (2019), senior fellow for PBLWorks, developed the following strategies and tips for PBL grading in conjunction with several PBLWorks National Faculty members:

- *Adjust expectations.* You don't need to reinvent your entire grading system, but you'll likely need to adjust community expectations (e.g., from students, parents, teachers) regarding homework and graded assignments.
- *Prioritize formative assessment.* Emphasize formative assessment to provide students with ongoing feedback without grades.

- *Grade separate assessments.* Assign separate grades or scores to each major summative assessment or product to avoid overreliance on a single grade.
- *Weight individual work.* Give greater weight to individual work to ensure fairness and address concerns from high-achieving students.
- *Vary assessment methods.* Incorporate traditional measures like quizzes and tests alongside written assignments to assess individual content knowledge. Experiment with assessment approaches like peer review, screencast feedback (viewing student work on a screen to gather feedback from classmates), and credit/no-credit assignments.
- *Involve students in assessment.* Have students participate in creating rubrics and self-assessing their work.
- *Utilize rubrics.* Create rubrics early in the project to clearly define quality criteria, ensure students understand expectations, and provide consistent feedback.
- *Focus on process over product.* In some cases, the process of completing a project may be more important than the final product.
- *Use feedback effectively.* Use grades as feedback opportunities rather than just summative indicators.

We recommend you start by encouraging the use of standards-aligned rubrics as a tool for growth within projects, as this practice allows teachers to address many of the strategies and tips concurrently. In PBL, students demonstrate their learning through the development of products, which require them to apply their knowledge and skills in an authentic context. In these performance assessments, teachers will see the tightest alignment to disciplinary standards and the clearest evidence of developing content knowledge and success skills. A well-designed project rubric communicates criteria for achieving the learning goals (both standards and success skills) that students are expected to know, do, and reflect on throughout a unit. Such a rubric can also anchor teachers' and students' assessment of individual and group products, ideally subsequent to refinement using critique and revision protocols with peers, experts, and the teacher.

Project rubrics can be applied to performance assessments at strategic times to gather evidence of student learning throughout the unit. This allows teachers to develop their knowledge of students and ensure that every student is experiencing the appropriate levels of cognitive demand.

Rubrics are also an essential strategy for student agency, as they allow students to understand their progress and provide a scaffold to help them develop personalized plans for improvement and refinement.

Here are some suggestions for ways to build your capacity to support teachers in the development and use of well-designed rubrics that are aligned to learning goals and products:

- *Support the development and usage of common rubrics* for agreed-upon graduate profile outcomes and success skills. For inspiration, consult PBLWorks's collection of evidence-based rubrics for common success skills (www.pblworks.org/research/success-skills-rubrics).
- *Review exemplars of rubrics and performance assessments.* Look for commonalities and become familiar with key components.
- *Review your grading system and policies* to ensure they facilitate teachers' use of rubrics as assessments for and of learning. Although it's not the only method that works with PBL, a standards-based grading system is usually more aligned with deeper learning assessment practices.
- *Start conversations* with teachers and other instructional leaders about how you know what students know and can do. Discuss the importance of having multiple and varied forms of evidence of learning at the classroom and school level.
- *Support exhibitions and presentations of learning* anchored in project work where students have to know, do, and reflect on their learning.

You may be wondering if it is actually possible to systemically embed assessment practices for deeper learning to improve students' outcomes. The case study below highlights how Envision Schools, which Bob co-founded, made it happen.

Leadership Story: Performance Assessments and Rubrics

Dressed to the nines, Alexis, a senior at an Envision School in Oakland, California, stands in front of a panel of teachers, counselors, administrators, and other school staff explaining how his Political Campaign Project analytical paper demonstrates his knowledge of U.S. Government content standards, his ability to write at a college-ready level, and his critical thinking and effective communication skills. To do so, Alexis compares specific examples from his essay to the standards addressed in Envision Schools' Critical Thinking and Communication Rubric. The panel questions and probes Alexis's thinking with hard, evidence-based questions. After conferring as a panel, they certify that Alexis has met the criteria for graduation based on his performance and defense of his work.

Located in Northern California, Envision Schools include three secondary-level charter schools: City Arts & Leadership Academy, Envision Academy, and Impact Academy of Arts & Technology. At Envision Schools, 99 percent of graduates are accepted to college, 75 percent of first-generation students attend college, and college attendees attain an 84 percent first-year college persistence rate.

Co-founded by Bob in 2002, Envision Schools provide a model of how to systemically embed assessment practices for deeper learning to improve student outcomes. The schools' graduate profiles are structured around the KDR framework: Graduates know the content and the discrete skills of their academic subjects, can do what typical college courses demand (research, analysis, inquiry), and have the ability to reflect, a habit of self-awareness and revision that sets them on the path of continued growth. What are the steps the schools took to reach these goals?

The leaders at Envision Schools started by working with teachers and the community to articulate and agree on graduate profile outcomes that reflected what they felt students needed to know and be able to do by the end of their time at Envision. The KDR framework came to be during this process. Students would demonstrate their content knowledge (know) on traditional assessments, apply the skills they were learning (do) through PBL, and focus on metacognition about their learning (reflect).

Once they agreed on graduate profile outcomes, the leaders at Envision partnered with the Stanford Center for Assessment, Learning, and Equity (SCALE) to build their capacity to develop a performance assessment system that supported students in demonstrating the application of academic skills and outcomes by producing college-ready work. They started by examining student work with two goals in mind. First, they identified what evidence students would need to submit to show they were college-ready for each subject area, agreed on what quality work looked like for those products, and invited feedback on these decisions from college professors. Second, they developed a variety of standards-aligned rubrics for each discipline that could be applied to various products. For example, in science, one rubric was designed for scientific inquiry and one for scientific analysis. SCALE took on the heavy lifting of rubric development to accelerate the process and avoid lengthy wordsmithing sessions. A set of rubrics was also developed for the graduate profile outcomes.

Leaders set clear expectations that teachers were required to use the rubrics when developing and teaching projects. They made time for teachers to engage in calibration sessions using student project work to apply and refine the rubrics and improve rating reliability. In addition to aligning projects with common outcomes and rubrics, Envision leaders put critical conditions in place to support the use of performance assessments. This meant making sure that teachers had common students and common planning time. It also meant developing common behavioral expectations for students, common processes such as using thinking routines in all classrooms, and common approaches to grading.

To round out their performance assessment system, Envision leaders also prioritized the development of a portfolio defense process to reinforce the expectation that students would learn to think critically, not merely regurgitate information and leverage test-taking strategies. Test-taking is an essential skill for students to acquire, but a test grade should not be the end goal of education. Instead, the goal should be for students to graduate with an arsenal of information they know deeply and skills they can use in future settings. Although Envision teachers employ multiple assessment types to ensure students achieve their learning goals (including in-class formative assessments, project based exhibitions, and standardized testing), their signature assessment method is the portfolio defense.

The portfolio defense process fully engages students in gaining new knowledge and skills (know), using the new content for authentic purposes (do), and thinking about their own learning (reflect). The defense is where they demonstrate how much they have learned and grown, what they have noticed about themselves in the process, and what they will need to improve to ensure a successful upper-division high school experience or success in college. In a portfolio defense, the student describes work they have done, presents artifacts that represent various skills and competencies, and connects the learning experience to their goals for the future.

In addition to the portfolio defense, Envision Schools students and teachers present their learning to the broader community at least twice a year. At Envision Academy in Oakland, California, Bob recently had a chance to listen to 9th and 10th grade students debrief their fall exhibition. The 9th graders presented their learning through digital media, telling their stories as learners and people. They presented in semiformal attire at an evening performance at school. They shared their poems and artwork not just with their teachers but also with their parents, siblings, grandparents, and other guests. During the class reflections, a teacher shared a story of one parent's tears of joy as she watched her son present his project. The 10th graders celebrated with "Academy Awards" for their performance of short, theatrical public service announcements on social and medical issues covered in their biology classes. The principal shared that two of the winners for Best Male Actor were students who came to Envision Academy struggling with skill gaps and low motivation. They were inspired to achieve by the project and the public performance.

Envision leaders and teachers know that talking about their learning—articulating it, reflecting on it, and internalizing it—engages students in the kind of assessment that continually reinforces skills, deepens knowledge, and prepares them for the future.

Capacity Building for Assessing Deeper Learning in Practice

To help you put your new knowledge into practice, here are some mini-trials that you can use to explore what it's like to build capacity for assessing deeper learning. We encourage you to try at least one thing from the list. Afterward, record your reflections and note any new insights you acquired.

- *Examine one or more exemplar PBL units* with a focus on the types and timing of assessments used in PBL.
- *Consider your building or district's current assessment reality* (e.g., summative grades) and ideal state (e.g., standards-aligned assessments, formative assessment, rubrics). What will progress look like, sound like, and feel like? What steps will you take to move closer to your ideal state?
- *Explore the PBLWorks success skills rubrics* (www.pblworks.org/research/success-skills-rubrics). Note how these rubrics help us envision learning on a continuum and consider how they would apply

to the outcomes we are looking for from PBL. Teachers will likely be more willing to try rubrics if they start by applying them to success skills instead of their content.

- Work with a teacher to determine the amount of time they spend grading and how that time can be better spent on planning lessons with formative assessments in mind.

Reflect

What did you try? What did you learn from your experience?

How has your view of your role in leading teachers regarding assessment of deeper learning shifted?

What are one to three actions you can take for quick wins to build the capacity for assessment and grading to support your vision for PBL?

Final Reflections

1. Revisit your original mental model of assessment for deeper learning. How does it connect to what you have read about building your capacity to lead for assessment in PBL? Did your thinking change at all? If so, in what ways?
2. Refer to the elements and leadership practices detailed in Figure 7.1. How do you rate yourself after learning more about assessment and grading practices for PBL? What are your strengths? Where are your opportunities to grow?
3. What specific aspects of your current school assessment practices align with the elements of capacity building for assessment of deeper learning? How might you expand on them?
4. Who are the assessment leaders on your campus? In other words, who naturally leans into the practices associated with assessment for deeper learning? What can you learn from them? How might you lift their practices in a way that inspires others?
5. Go back to the leadership story shared in the case study. In what ways did Bob and the other leaders at Envision build capacity for assessment in PBL? What lessons could you apply to your setting or practice?

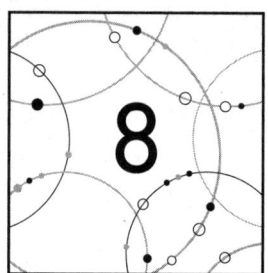

Measuring Impact for Continuous Improvement

I find that I am often driven by what feels like a good idea. You know, PBL seems like a really good idea. Continuous improvement work has challenged me to better articulate how we will know if the change we are trying is actually an improvement. Like, how would you know?

—Ben Daley, president, High Tech High Graduate School of Education

KNOW

As a school leader, you are highly aware of the need to collect data beyond test scores to tell a more holistic story of the learning that happens in your school. Lots of schools regularly collect a myriad of data that can paint a broader picture, but far too few intentionally build the capacity of teachers and school leaders to unpack and leverage these data for continuous improvement. Many underlying factors make this a challenging endeavor. For one, measures assessing student outcomes can be very broad, making it nearly impossible to determine school-level or implementation factors that might be causing shifts in the data over time. Second, schools are drowning in data, with little guidance or time to extract meaning that can drive storytelling and improvements. Finally, schools are often required to implement multiple initiatives at the behest of well-meaning district and state leaders who often expect an innovation or program to lead directly to educationally significant outcomes without understanding the importance of monitoring the quality of implementation or the enabling conditions needed for success. While we can't always avoid what we lovingly call the "full-plate syndrome," we have developed a way to help school leaders overcome some of these challenges by collecting, analyzing, and responding to a very specific data set that can help them better tell the story of and improve their PBL implementation.

> **Reflect**
>
> **What is your current mental model of using data to promote continuous improvement? What does it look like, sound like, and feel like?**

Over the past several years, PBLWorks has been working with our school and district partners to learn more about how to support schools with a continuous improvement process that includes systematically collecting evidence to track progress in implementing Gold Standard PBL to improve mastery of academic content and success skills for all students. As an outgrowth of this work, we have created a School PBL Evidence Framework (Wagner & Kingston, 2023; available at www.pblworks.org/school-pbl-evidence-framework-toolkit) designed to track the effective implementation of key indicators of PBL that "move the needle" on academic content and success skills. The framework is designed to be used throughout a school's PBL journey, from readiness to student outcomes, to provide ongoing data to support reflection, planning, and celebration.

This enables schools to formatively track progress on key indicators along the journey and collect summative student data to show what students know and can do due to their engagement in high-quality PBL. The framework is built on a set of three key assumptions:

1. *We need to use measures beyond test scores.* Standardized test scores are still upheld as the single measure of a school's success. Yet we know that students in PBL classrooms show improvement across a variety of student outcomes, including attendance, engagement, academic skills, creativity, critical thinking, collaboration, communication, self-directed learning, and much more (Condliffe et al., 2017; Duke et al., 2021; Saavedra et al., 2021). We need a broader set of measures to better tell the story of what students know and can do at the classroom, school, and district levels.

2. *Implementation matters.* Effective implementation is the key to the success and sustainability of any program, initiative, or practice. Implementation science research concludes that "using systematic methods and having data as feedback provides the opportunity to 'learn to learn' and become more effective and efficient with experience" (Fixsen et al., 2005, p. 72). A growing body of rigorous research confirms what we know: PBL is an effective innovation (Condliffe et al., 2017; Duke et al., 2021; Saavedra et al., 2021; Thomas, 2000). We also know that appropriate implementation and enabling conditions are essential for improved student outcomes (see Figure 8.1; Fixsen et al., 2005).

3. *It's a journey.* Improving student outcomes takes time and patience, and as with any change, the process requires support and intentionality. Using Gold Standard PBL as a core instructional practice across a school is a journey well worth taking. We conceptualized schoolwide PBL implementation as a trip, starting

Figure 8.1 Formula for Program Success

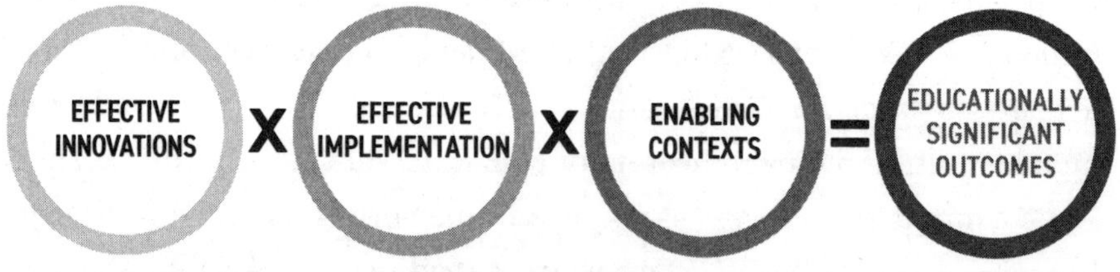

EFFECTIVE INNOVATIONS **X** EFFECTIVE IMPLEMENTATION **X** ENABLING CONTEXTS **=** EDUCATIONALLY SIGNIFICANT OUTCOMES

Source: From *School PBL Evidence Framework Toolkit* (p. 6), 2023, Buck Institute for Education. Copyright 2023 by Buck Institute for Education. Reprinted with permission.

with the end in mind: Where do we want to go? What do we want students to know and be able to do as a result of their experiences with high-quality PBL? Then, we worked our way backward: How will we know when we arrive at our ultimate destination? What are the key milestones that will tell us that we are making progress? Of all the things we could look for along the way, what matters most? And, finally, how do we know we are ready to take the journey? What do we need to have in place? We urge you to think about your own PBL journey in this way.

School PBL Evidence Framework Components

The School PBL Evidence Framework (Wagner & Kingston, 2023) has three components: readiness, leading indicators, and academic and success skills (see Figure 8.2). The *readiness* criteria help leaders know whether they are ready to launch a PBL initiative scaling Gold Standard PBL across classrooms. The *leading indicators* criteria track the status of PBL implementation and identify key conditions that need to be in place to promote academic and success skills, including school leadership, teaching and learning, and student experiences. The *academic and success skills* criteria reference mastery of student outcomes achieved through Gold Standard PBL, including standards-aligned academic content and success skills (i.e., critical thinking, collaboration, communication, creativity, and self-directed learning), to evaluate student learning progress.

Ultimately, we aim to support PBL school leaders in becoming more comfortable and effective in planning for and leading an ongoing reflection, adaptation, and growth process to improve student learning outcomes through Gold Standard PBL. As the instructional leader of your school, you will need to be able to do the following:

- *Collect and analyze evidence* to track and improve progress on graduate profile outcomes and implementation.
- *Design and lead short continuous improvement cycles* focused on the rate and effectiveness of implementing Gold Standard PBL experiences.
- *Anticipate and strategically solve challenges and barriers* to effective implementation of Gold Standard PBL.

Figure 8.2 School PBL Evidence Framework

READINESS	LEADING INDICATORS			ACADEMIC AND SUCCESS SKILLS
Are we ready?	Is our Implementation on track?			Are we making progress?
School Leadership	**PBL School Leadership**	**PBL School Conditions**	**PBL Design and Teaching**	**High-Quality PBL (HQPBL) Student Experiences**	**Academic and Success Skills**
Vision for deeper learning (and/or graduate profile)	% of leadership team who report that they . . .	% of schools with . . .	% of teachers who report that they . . .	% of students, including those furthest from opportunity, whose teachers report engaging in . . .	% of students, including those furthest from opportunity, who report or demonstrate . . .
Established school leadership team responsible for school-wide PBL implementation	• Are confident in their ability to lead Gold Standard PBL implementation at their school *Measured by PBL Implementation Pulse Surveys (minimally quarterly)*	• Instructional schedules with blocks of time for students to engage in Gold Standard PBL (equivalent of at least 75 minutes twice a week) *Measured by PBL Implementation Pulse Surveys (minimally quarterly)*	• Understand Gold Standard PBL Essential Project Design Elements *Measured by PBL Implementation Pulse Surveys (minimally quarterly)*	• At least 2 Gold Standard PBL projects each year *Measured by project tracking tool*	• Critical thinking
Teachers	• Have the support they need to lead the implementation of Gold Standard PBL well *Measured by PBL Implementation Pulse Surveys (minimally quarterly)*	• Teachers who have the collaborative planning time they need to design projects and to effectively use Gold Standard PBL Project Based Teaching Practices (at least equivalent to 6 hrs/month) *Measured by PBL Implementation Pulse Surveys (minimally quarterly)*	• Facilitate PBL Using Gold Standard PBL Project Based Teaching Practices with confidence *Measured by PBL Implementation Pulse Surveys (minimally quarterly)*	% of teachers and/or students, including those furthest from opportunity, who report that students . . .	• Collaboration
Cadre of teachers who are PBL champions or willing to lead PBL				• Engage in projects aligned to the HQPBL criteria *Measured by teacher and student HQPBL surveys*	• Communication
					• Creativity
	• Believe that PBL, when done well, can be used as a primary teaching method for all students, including those furthest from opportunity *Measured by PBL Implementation Pulse Surveys (minimally quarterly)*	• Teachers who engage in at least 14 hours of PBL coaching and/or support *Measured by PBL Implementation Pulse Surveys (minimally quarterly)*	• Believe that Gold Standard PBL can be used as a primary teaching method for all students, including those furthest from opportunity *Measured by PBL Implementation Pulse Surveys (minimally quarterly)*	• Engage in at least 2 student exhibitions or presentations of learning each year *Measured by PBL Implementation Pulse Surveys (minimally quarterly)*	• Self-direction
					• Mastery of academic core content
					Measured by success skills rubrics and survey of success skills

Source: From *School PBL Evidence Framework Toolkit* (p. 13), by K. Wagner and S. Kingston, 2023, Buck Institute for Education. Copyright 2023 by Buck Institute for Education. Adapted with permission.

Figure 8.3 identifies three elements related to continuous improvement that can accelerate the effective implementation of PBL, along with their associated leadership practices.

Collection, Analysis, and Use of Data on Success Skills

Although research shows that high-quality PBL positively affects student outcomes in all core content areas and for all students (Condliffe et al., 2017; Duke et al., 2021; Saavedra et al., 2021), it is important to collect school-level data related to both academic and success skills to understand and be able to tell the story of how PBL is influencing outcomes for your students. We know that data collection is time-consuming. Making sure that the data you are collecting are meaningful is key to successful and sustained data analysis and reporting efforts. We suggest starting by focusing on just one academic skill and two success skills. For the academic skill, choose one that matters to your community and can tell a story about student success in your school's PBL journey. Determining which success skills to focus on often requires substantial grappling. We suggest focusing on ones commonly found in graduate profiles, likely to be developed in projects, and able to be measured using PBLWorks research-based rubrics for evaluating the following success skills:

- Critical thinking
- Collaboration
- Complex communication
- Creativity
- Self-directed learning

Once you have determined which academic and success skills to prioritize, examine your school's current reality by collecting and analyzing baseline student data on the selected skills. Assessing your students' starting points with your leadership team promotes collaborative reflection while also providing a point of comparison for future data. We strongly recommend disaggregating data to ensure you are making progress with all groups of students. As you build your data collection plan, consider the following:

Figure 8.3 Measuring Impact for Continuous Improvement: Elements and Leadership Practices

Element	Leadership Practice
Collection, analysis, and use of data on success skills Rating: _____	I have put systems in place to collect, analyze, and use data to show progress on what students know and can do as a result of PBL.
Implementation management Rating: _____	I have put a system in place to monitor the implementation of PBL schoolwide, anticipate challenges, and address current barriers to effective implementation.
Continuous improvement processes Rating: _____	Our leadership team and teacher teams regularly use short-cycle improvement processes, including information-gathering strategies such as classroom walkthroughs and learning walks, to evaluate and adjust the implementation of Gold Standard PBL.

On a scale of 1 ("I have not yet explored this") to 4 ("This is central to my practice"), rate yourself on each leadership practice to help determine your readiness to lead continuous improvement efforts at your school and decide where to focus your efforts.

After you've read the chapter, use the space below to reflect on what concrete steps you can take to collect and apply data to improve your school's implementation of PBL.

Copyright © 2018 Buck Institute for Education. Reprinted with permission.

- What are your priority academic and success skills? What data do you already collect related to them?
- What readiness and implementation indicators from the School PBL Evidence Framework (Figure 8.2) make the most sense for your school? How do the indicators align with indicators related to a school improvement plan, accreditation, or other accountability requirements? What additional indicators might you need to consider?
- How will you establish a baseline for student work?
- How will you set up a data collection and analysis plan to monitor growth and progress at the classroom, grade or subject, and school levels?

Many schools we work with have a plan to use rubrics to review a cross section of student work regularly. You can do this in several ways, depending on your context. For example, if you lead a school new to PBL, you could have teachers submit student work samples demonstrating learning related to the focus on academic or success skills. Reassure teachers that this review is not evaluative but a way to get a snapshot of students' current reality. If your school is more experienced with PBL, you can use student work from teacher-developed projects that center on the selected academic and success skills.

Here are some more suggestions to aid you in collecting, analyzing, and using data for continuous improvement:

- *Review the data you currently collect* related to academic and success skills. What might be most informative and useful to leverage as you embark on or continue your PBL journey?
- *Take advantage of existing processes to review student work* or portfolios. For example, if your school already engages in student-led conferences, pull sample student work from those to gather baseline data on your selected academic or success skills.
- *Build on existing momentum.* For example, if your school is focusing on literacy, choosing to prioritize communication as a success skill and writing as an academic skill makes sense.
- *Review your current data collection plan* and compare it with the Sample Data Collection Plan in Appendix C. If you don't have a data collection plan, use the sample plan as a template to create one.

Implementation Management

As mentioned earlier, implementation matters. Too often, school leaders implement an innovation and rely solely on student outcome data to determine whether it is effective. If the innovation doesn't produce immediate results, they quickly abandon it, seeking the next best thing rather than exploring why they may not have realized the desired impact. PBL leaders know that change takes time and expect typical implementation dips in outcome data. We encourage schools we work with to focus on monitoring the implementation of PBL by tracking the leading indicators identified in the School PBL Evidence Framework:

- PBL School Leadership
  - Do leaders feel confident in their ability to lead Gold Standard PBL in their school?
  - Do leaders have the support they need to lead the implementation of Gold Standard PBL well?
  - Do leaders believe that PBL, when done well, can be used as a primary teaching method for all students, including those furthest from opportunity?
- PBL School Conditions
  - Do students have blocks of time to engage in Gold Standard PBL (equivalent to at least 75 minutes twice a week)?
  - Do teachers have at least six hours a month of collaborative planning time to design or adapt projects and effectively use the Gold Standard PBL Project Based Teaching Practices?
  - Do teachers engage in at least 14 hours of PBL coaching and support during the school year?
- PBL Design and Teaching
  - Do teachers understand the Gold Standard PBL Essential Project Design Elements?
  - Do teachers facilitate PBL using the Gold Standard PBL Project Based Teaching Practices with confidence?
  - Do teachers believe Gold Standard PBL can be a primary teaching method for all students, including those furthest from opportunity?
- PBL Student Experiences
  - Do all students engage in at least two Gold Standard PBL projects each year?

- Do all students engage in projects that are aligned with high-quality PBL criteria?
- Do all students engage in at least two student exhibitions or presentations of learning each year?

You may have noticed that the above questions align with the recommendations and ideas emphasized in previous chapters. This is intentional. We want to ensure we measure what we implement. Each question also aligns with a measurable indicator found in our PBL Implementation Pulse Survey (Appendix D). We encourage you to administer this survey to teachers early in your journey to obtain baseline data and then on a regular, quarterly basis.

Principals who piloted our School PBL Evidence Framework noted that the PBL Implementation Pulse Survey was the most useful tool in their PBL journey. Tracking implementation periodically helps leaders anticipate challenges and address systemic inertia that often impedes or derails innovation. Peter Senge (2006) describes this process as reinforcing and balancing loops. The premise is that all organizations, like organisms, are designed to conserve (protect) themselves from outside forces. These built-in protections are the balancing loops that keep the organization in status quo, but they can be viewed as resistance to change. In contrast, reinforcing loops amplify change or growth.

Consider what practices are helping to grow or reinforce PBL implementation at your school and what is limiting it. How might you leverage PBL Implementation Pulse Survey results to promote reinforcing loops and better understand and address the balancing loops, or barriers limiting PBL implementation? For example, the schedule can be a reinforcing or balancing loop, depending on how it's structured. A schedule that allows six hours of teacher collaboration each month would be reinforcing; one that has students engaging in PBL for only 45 minutes twice a week would probably be a balancing or limiting loop.

While PBL Implementation Pulse Survey results offer insight into challenges and barriers to PBL implementation at your school, it is also crucial to regularly engage in conversations with teachers and students to determine what is working well and what might need your attention. This engagement can take the form of one-to-one conversations, focus groups, or even a chalk talk in a staff meeting, where teachers silently build on each other's ideas to strengthen implementation. As you work to address barriers, find ways to share and spread any bright spots you learn about. In doing so, you will create more robust reinforcing loops and foster conditions to strengthen implementation.

Here are some steps to take as you manage PBL implementation in your school:

- *Review the PBL Implementation Pulse Survey* in Appendix D. What do you notice? What do you wonder? What could you learn from administering the survey?
- *Reflect on current or anticipated PBL implementation challenges.* How might you better understand them or check your thinking?
- *Assess your school's current status.* Are any teachers, grade levels, or departments engaging in practices that align well with PBL implementation? How might you learn from them and spread or scale the practices to others?
- *Consider the barriers you need to address* to support the growth of PBL in your school. What quick wins can you focus on first?

Continuous Improvement Processes

In addition to administering the PBL Implementation Pulse Survey and having focused conversations, we strongly encourage school leaders to use additional information-gathering strategies to get a more holistic picture and additional data points to evaluate and adjust their implementation of Gold Standard PBL practices. One strategy is to engage in classroom walkthroughs focused on one or two Gold Standard PBL Project Based Teaching Practices at a time (ideally, ones being explored during teachers' professional development). Walkthroughs can be short and might include one or two other leaders from your school. Use the Project Based Teaching Practices Rubric (Appendix B) to look for evidence of the indicators associated with one of the practices and then conduct a structured post-observation dialogue with leadership colleagues or the teacher. Make sure to communicate the purpose and timing of the walkthroughs to the teachers you will be observing in advance.

Leadership learning walks can also be quite effective in helping you see what you can't see. Sometimes, as leaders, we are too close to the work. A set of fresh eyes, especially those of a trusted leader colleague, can provide fresh insight. As described in Chapter 6, a leadership learning walk consists of a small group of principals meeting at a school site. The host principal shares evidence of one aspect of PBL implementation to gain insight from their peers on how to improve on it. This evidence-sharing could take many forms, including reviewing project planners or student work, talking to teachers or students about PBL, or visiting classrooms to look for a particular PBL component (e.g., student voice, the focus success skill, student engagement). Next, visiting principals comment on what they noticed, liked, and wondered about while the host principal listens. Finally, the host principal reflects and shares any new insights they gained with the group. Principals we work with tell us that engaging in leadership learning walks is one of the most powerful professional learning experiences they have engaged in because it leverages the wisdom of their peers and is rooted in their own school's context.

Both strategies can provide additional timely and essential data to supplement PBL Implementation Pulse Survey results. As you build your data collection plan, ensure that you examine the results of your efforts using a short-cycle improvement process like the one outlined in Figure 8.4. Short-cycle processes allow you to better respond to challenges and

Figure 8.4 PBL Continuous Improvement Process

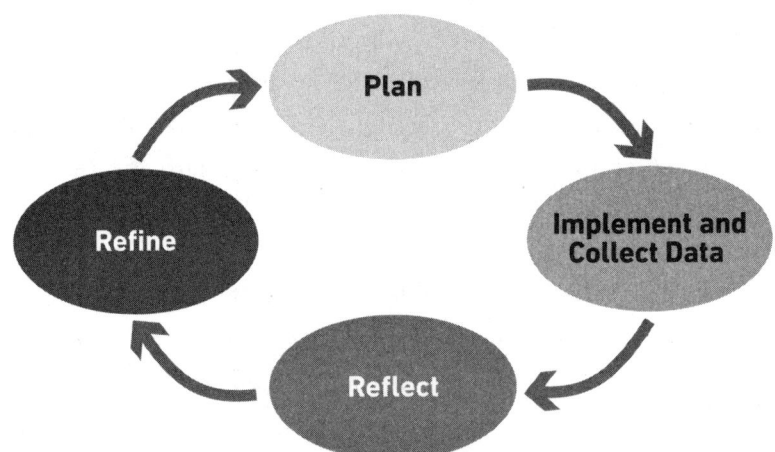

Source: From *School PBL Evidence Framework Toolkit* (p. 14), 2023, Buck Institute for Education. Copyright 2023 by Buck Institute for Education. Reprinted with permission.

scale emerging bright spots to accelerate PBL implementation efforts. Let's break down each phase more clearly.

Plan

The planning phase answers the question "Are we ready?" During this phase, you will want to determine readiness for PBL and ensure that leadership has taken the necessary steps to prepare for a successful PBL journey. During this phase, identify and collect baseline data on prioritized academic and success skills.

Implement and Collect Data

This phase answers the questions "Where are we now?" and "How are we progressing on our PBL journey?" During this phase, you implement your PBL plan, provide adequate time for the plan to proceed, and collect data to assess your progress. A well-thought-out data collection plan ensures the ongoing, regular evaluation of leading indicator data. Avoid the tendency to overcollect data, as too-frequent collection intervals will not reflect the impact of improvements or meaningful change. Regular assessment of your school's current reality promotes team reflection on what students know and can do and the conditions in place (or not) for successful PBL implementation.

Reflect

The reflecting phase answers the question "How is it going?" In this phase, the PBL school leadership cadre or implementation team reflects on the data using structured protocols. Observations should be factual and based on the data. Using protocols such as the one reproduced in Figure 8.5 creates a safer space for sharing as well as a culture of collaboration, engagement, and buy-in that is vital to the continuous improvement of PBL implementation (Killion, 2018). Protocols promote listening, reflection, and equity of voice, allowing for collective meaning-making. Many data protocols can be adapted for your unique team and context.

Refine

This phase answers the question "What might we do differently?" During refinement, conversation turns to inferences and recommendations based

Figure 8.5 Protocol for Reflecting on Data

Steps	Task	Time
Review protocol	Facilitator reviews protocol steps and time.	5 minutes
Look at data	Look at the quarterly results across the PBL conditions: PBL school leadership, PBL school conditions, PBL design and teaching, and HQPBL student experiences.	10 minutes
Round 1: Wins	Each team member shares an observation related to PBL implementation wins.	5 minutes
Round 2: Areas for growth	Each team member shares an observation related to PBL implementation growth.	5 minutes
Round 3: Equity issues	Each team member shares any equity issue/gap evident in the data.	5 minutes
Round 4: Needs	Each team member identifies what is still needed to grow PBL.	5 minutes
Final round: Surprises and questions	Team members share surprises and questions that emerged from the data review.	10 minutes
		Total: 45 minutes

Source: From *School PBL Evidence Framework Toolkit* (p. 21), 2023, Buck Institute for Education. Copyright 2023 by Buck Institute for Education. Adapted with permission.

on the observations made during the previous phase. The goal is to add value to the data through reflection and inquiry before shifting the focus to actionable recommendations or next steps. Consider the leading indicator data you collected and analyzed. Do the data point to an initial area of focus for professional learning? Do they point to a condition that needs to be addressed sooner rather than later? During this phase, we strongly encourage you to pick one thing to focus on to deepen your PBL implementation. Keep in mind that it's essential to dig into the root cause of an issue before rushing to solutions or improvements. Protocols such as the one reproduced in Figure 8.6 can help you better identify actions that address the cause rather than the symptoms.

As you work on practicing continuous improvement processes, consider the following questions:

Figure 8.6 Protocol for Refining Plans Based on Data

Steps	Action	Time
Review protocol	Facilitator reviews protocol steps and time.	5 minutes
Reflect	Individually, silently reflect on the observations shared during the Reflecting on Data protocol and these guiding questions: • **What we know:** What do these data seem to tell us? What do they not tell us? Are there triangulation points from various stakeholders? Gaps? What assumptions are we making? • **What we need to know:** What else would we need to know? • **What else is at play:** What else might be influencing the results? What factors were at play? How influential were those factors?	10 minutes
Discuss	Using the guiding questions, discuss what you noticed during the Reflecting on Data protocol.	15 minutes
Refine	Based on your discussion, identify and document actions you will take to progress on your PBL journey: Are there immediate needs that need to be addressed? How might we improve the enabling conditions aligned to these indicators? For whom? How? What strategies might be most effective? What resources are available?	20 minutes
Plan	Update PBL implementation plans, define focus areas, and/or revisit your data collection plan. Begin data collection cycle again.	5 minutes
		Total: 55 minutes

Source: From *School PBL Evidence Framework Toolkit* (p. 24), 2023, Buck Institute for Education. Copyright 2023 by Buck Institute for Education. Adapted with permission.

- What current strategies are in place at your school to gather information on everyday teaching and learning? How do they align with or differ from the classroom walkthroughs or leader learning walks described above?
- Reflect on your current short-cycle improvement processes. How do they align with or differ from what you are learning?

- Are any teachers, grade levels, or departments in your school engaging in effective short-cycle improvement processes? How might you learn from them and spread or scale their practices to others?
- How could you better include students and teachers in your short-cycle improvement processes? What would be the value in doing so?

Continuous improvement can be hard work, but it is the most critical work to do to ensure equitable outcomes for students. When done well, it helps you better understand your teachers and the student experience and be more prepared to identify and address PBL implementation challenges. Providing regular opportunities for student and teacher feedback and responding with positive and supportive actions elevates teacher and student voice and strengthens the culture in support of PBL. As you work to identify actions to refine PBL implementation in your school, ask yourself how you can best foster teacher and student agency. How might they help you address implementation barriers? When and how can student and teacher ideas help inform improvements? Engaging in this work will also help you ensure that every student is getting access to high-quality PBL so they feel known, experience cognitive demand, develop comprehensive literacy skills, and benefit from shared power at both the classroom and school level.

Let's turn to a case study to learn how one leader leveraged continuous improvement processes to address the "messy middle" of PBL implementation.

PBL Leadership Story: Continuous Improvement Processes

Kamaliʻi Elementary in Kihei, Hawaiʻi, began their PBL journey in the spring of 2019 and maintained it through the virtual learning period necessitated by the COVID-19 pandemic. By the 2022–23 school year, the Kamaliʻi team was ready to dial up its PBL practices and push through the "messy middle" of schoolwide PBL implementation. After returning to in-person instruction, the school's leadership and faculty were determined not only to resume their PBL journey but also to dig deeper and focus on delivering Gold Standard PBL experiences to every student.

Diving into PBLWorks's PBL School Evidence Framework Toolkit, the Kamaliʻi leadership team, led by Principal Cynthia Rothdeutsch and Academic Coach Kacie Seitz, quickly identified leading indicators and simple data collection methods to gather evidence of their current reality. They started the school year by evaluating teachers' understanding of the Gold Standard PBL Essential Project Design Elements using the PBL Implementation Pulse Survey. Considering their progress in their PBL journey, existing school data, and the survey results, the leadership team identified two Essential Project Design Elements as the focus for the year: reflection, and critique and revision. Leaning into their goal of differentiated support, the team reflected on data by grade level to provide targeted support during team planning and professional learning time. Impressively, their actions resulted in a significant increase in the number of teachers who reported they had felt confident enough to independently facilitate reflection (from 26 to 58 percent) and critique and revision (from 22 to 50 percent) by the end of the school year. The leadership team attributed their success to keeping their focus targeted and consistent, in addition to the following actions:

- *Sharing power with a PBL cadre.* The PBL Cadre included a group of volunteer PBL champions who represented each grade level. These teachers took part in early learning, provided feedback, and supported PBL communications and messaging throughout the school.
- *Collecting data with a commitment to transparency.* To monitor their progress consistently, the team designated a set time for teachers to complete the PBL Implementation Pulse Survey each quarter. To build coherence and trust, the school leadership team shared the PBL Implementation Pulse Survey data with the entire staff to reflect and plan for the next quarter. The team handled data dips by trusting that, with a deeper understanding of the prioritized practices, teachers would become more reflective and think more critically about their practice.
- *Engaging in ongoing professional learning.* Various professional learning opportunities were provided throughout the year, from formal workshops and courses with PBLWorks to sessions facilitated by the Kamaliʻi staff featuring targeted readings, protocols, and resources related to reflection and critique and revision.

- *Conducting classroom walkthroughs.* Visiting every classroom allowed the leadership team to engage with students and observe PBL in action. They also supported teachers and provided time for them to observe key Project Based Teaching Practices modeled by colleagues.

Principal Rothdeutsch is fortunate that her district invested in supporting school leaders with ongoing training on how to lead for PBL. She also applied for and was accepted into the Hawai'i Innovative Leader Network, a multiyear PBL School Leader Network focused on building the capacity of Hawai'i's school leaders in PBL. Principal Rothdeutsch participated wholeheartedly in these sessions and, with the support of her PBL leadership team, immediately implemented the strategies she learned. She regularly shared the school's journey at conferences and other meetings, where she also gained new insight and feedback from experts and colleagues. Most importantly, she regularly gathered data, formally and informally, and led thoughtful conversations using data analysis protocols. These practices allowed her to quickly respond to PBL implementation challenges with thoughtful solutions.

Measuring Impact for Continuous Improvement in Practice

To help you put your new knowledge into practice, here are some mini-trials you can use to explore what it's like to lead for continuous improvement for PBL. We encourage you to try at least one thing from either list. Afterward, record your reflections and note any new insights you acquired.

Individual Actions

1. *Download PBLWorks's School PBL Evidence Framework Toolkit* at www.pblworks.org/school-pbl-evidence-framework-toolkit. What insights do you gain from reading through the toolkit? How might you introduce the framework to others at your school? Who would you start with? What would a conversation or meeting with others about the framework look like, sound like, and feel like?

2. *Review* the readiness, leading indicators, and academic and success skills components of the School PBL Evidence Framework (Figure

8.2). How do they compare to the data you already collect? How ready do you think you are to implement PBL schoolwide? How do you think your school would fare on the implementation and student outcome indicators if you were to gather data today?

Collaborative Actions (Ideally with the PBL Leadership Cadre)

1. *Share the School PBL Evidence Framework Toolkit* with your leadership team and discuss potential benefits and challenges related to using it. How might you address those challenges? How might you leverage the tools and information in the toolkit to accelerate your school's PBL implementation?
2. During a PLC or staff meeting, *invite teachers to self-assess their instruction* using the Project Based Teaching Practices Rubric (Appendix B) and then set a personal focus goal for the next quarter. Provide resources and support for them to work individually with a coach or as a team on their chosen practice, and then have them re-assess at the end of a project or quarter to evaluate their growth.
3. *Sit with a grade-level or subject-area team* as they practice using a protocol to look for evidence of a prioritized academic or success skill in student work (PBL or not). This asset-based, low-stakes approach creates an opportunity for meaningful conversations, provides practice in facilitating a student work protocol, and gets teachers talking about student work.

Reflect

What did you try? What did you learn from your experience?

How has your view of your role as a continuous improvement leader for PBL shifted?

What are one to three actions you can take for quick wins to strengthen your approach to continuous improvement to advance PBL successfully in your school?

Final Reflections

1. Look back at your original mental model of measuring impact for continuous improvement. How does it connect to what you read in this chapter? Did your mental model change? If so, in what ways? If not, why not?
2. Refer to Figure 8.3 and your initial self-assessment of how you measure impact for continuous improvement. Using the same 1–4 rating scale, with 1 being "I have not yet explored this" and 4 being "This is central to my practice," how do you rate yourself after learning more about the practices? What are your strengths? Where are your opportunities to grow?
3. What specific aspects of your current reality align with the elements of continuous improvement for PBL? How might you expand or improve on these?
4. Go back to the leadership story shared earlier in the chapter. How did the leadership team leverage continuous improvement practices to strengthen PBL implementation in their school? What lessons could you apply in your setting or practice?

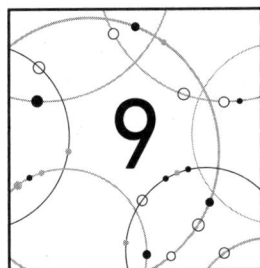

Translating PBL Leadership Practices for District Leaders

There's a real sense of self-empowerment because the kids can see themselves more and feel like active agents in their learning. . . . That experience can just completely change a student's trajectory, in terms of their engagement with the educational system.

—Rosanna Mucetti, superintendent,
Napa Valley Unified School District, California

As described in Chapter 1, our theory of action starts with the belief that leaders need a specific set of knowledge, skills, and dispositions about how to lead for PBL so they can create the conditions and build the capacity for teachers to be able to implement Gold Standard PBL consistently and effectively for a positive change in student success skills and academic outcomes. Although school leaders are primarily responsible for creating the conditions to enable Gold Standard PBL, district leaders play an equally important role in establishing coherence. What do we mean by coherence, and what does the research tell us about why it is critical?

> **Reflect**
> **What is your mental model of your role as a district leader supporting PBL? How do you envision that support in action?**

According to the RAND Corporation (Berglund et al., 2024), a coherent instructional system aligns curriculum, assessment, professional development, and instructional materials to support student learning. Their research emphasizes that such systems feature consistency and clarity in educational expectations, aiding teachers in delivering effective instruction. More coherent instructional systems support teacher confidence, while incoherence evokes frustration and anxiety.

As an example, the Learning Policy Institute's research (Willis et al., 2022) shows that performance assessments—a key feature of PBL—promote coherence and student-centered learning. The Learning Policy Institute emphasizes the need for policies and structures that enable performance-based assessments that align with deeper learning outcomes. At PBLWorks, we go one step further by advocating for policies and structures that support deep and sustained implementation of all aspects of PBL, as outlined in our District Logic Model (Figure 9.1). This means that district leaders need to be constantly focused on creating "swing."

In the novel *The Boys in the Boat*, Daniel James Brown describes "swing" as a state of perfect harmony among rowers: "It's called swing when all eight are rowing in such perfect unison, and no single action is out of sync with the rest of the boat" (Brown, 2014, p. 161). District leaders are uniquely responsible for ensuring that school leaders and teachers

Figure 9.1 PBLWorks District Logic Model

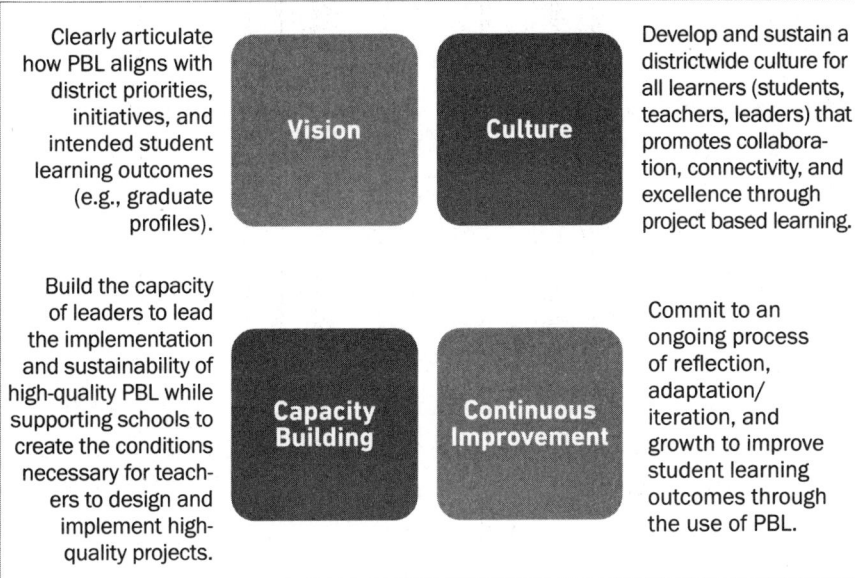

Clearly articulate how PBL aligns with district priorities, initiatives, and intended student learning outcomes (e.g., graduate profiles).

Develop and sustain a districtwide culture for all learners (students, teachers, leaders) that promotes collaboration, connectivity, and excellence through project based learning.

Build the capacity of leaders to lead the implementation and sustainability of high-quality PBL while supporting schools to create the conditions necessary for teachers to design and implement high-quality projects.

Commit to an ongoing process of reflection, adaptation/iteration, and growth to improve student learning outcomes through the use of PBL.

Copyright © 2019 Buck Institute for Education. Reprinted with permission.

feel like the school system's vision, culture, professional learning, and policies/programs for continuous improvement are aligned. The PBLWorks District Logic Model outlines at the highest level the steps district leaders must take to create "swing" for PBL.

To support the District Logic Model, we have identified a set of district outcomes, one for each domain, designed to accelerate effective implementation. Congruent with our Leadership Theory of Action, each domain specifies knowledge, skills, practices, dispositions, and implementation structures needed to support leaders in creating the conditions and ecosystem for successfully scaling PBL across the district. Let's start with the vision domain.

Vision

Chapter 3 emphasizes the importance of developing a North Star for PBL. Like the school leader, district leaders need to consider their own "why" for PBL as they work toward the outcome of developing a clear vision for the district that includes Gold Standard PBL and promotes student success in college, career, and life, especially for traditionally marginalized students. Figure 9.2 outlines specific knowledge and structures leaders should prioritize as they start or deepen an initiative to scale PBL districtwide.

PBL district leaders should work with the entire school system community to develop a clear and compelling vision for their graduates that outlines the skills and dispositions that educators, parents, community members, and business leaders agree are essential. In Chapter 3, we shared a list of the most common skills and dispositions gleaned from reviewing hundreds of these vision statements, often called graduate profiles, learner profiles, or portraits of a graduate. PBL district leaders should facilitate community and school sessions to gather input and eventually reach a consensus on the vision across stakeholders to be adopted by the district school board. This vision should reflect the "why" for implementing Gold Standard PBL. District leaders are then responsible for clearly communicating how Gold Standard PBL leads to success in college, career, and life for all students, as well as how it serves and aligns with other district initiatives.

We have seen the most significant progress in implementing and scaling PBL across the school system when district leaders make the commitment that every student will experience at least two high-quality PBL

Figure 9.2 District Leader Outcome, Practices, and Implementation Structures: Vision

Outcome	Develop a clear vision that includes Gold Standard PBL and promotes student success in college, career, and life, especially for students furthest from opportunity.
Knowledge, skills, practices, and dispositions	• Articulate a public commitment to Gold Standard PBL and a vision for how it serves and aligns with other district initiatives. • Advocate for all students to experience Gold Standard PBL with high expectations and support for their success.
Structures for implementation	• Make a public commitment (e.g., school board policy, district strategic plan) that every student will experience at least two high-quality PBL experiences every year. • Agree upon a set of student outcomes (e.g., graduate profile) related to academic success, success skills, and student empowerment. • Devise a strategy for rolling out and scaling PBL as a vehicle for students to achieve graduate profile outcomes (e.g., scaling map).

Copyright © 2019 Buck Institute for Education. Reprinted with permission.

experiences every year. Successful leaders move beyond rhetoric to concrete actions, such as crafting a board policy with such a requirement or incorporating PBL implementation actions into the district strategic plan. They are also intentional and thoughtful about where and how they start to scale PBL across the district.

We have worked with districts that have done a fabulous job of (1) creating a graduate profile, (2) articulating a compelling vision for Gold Standard PBL, (3) offering professional learning for the entire district, and (4) creating a districtwide expectation that all teachers will implement two PBL units a year, only to be disappointed when only some teachers follow through. Leaders in these districts are perplexed that despite taking steps to craft the vision, develop the culture, and build capacity, only some students get to experience high-quality PBL sometimes, and many students don't get to at all. We explain this phenomenon using the diffusion of innovations theory, introduced by sociologist Everett Rogers (2003). The theory explains how innovations spread through social systems, categorizing adopters into five groups: innovators, early adopters, early majority, late majority, and laggards. Following is how these category members interact with PBL implementation:

- *Innovators* are the first to adopt PBL, often motivated by a passion for new teaching methods or philosophies.
- *Early adopters* embrace PBL relatively early, often becoming advocates and sharing their experiences with colleagues.
- *Early majority* teachers adopt PBL once they see evidence of its effectiveness and acceptance from their peers.
- *Late majority* teachers are more cautious, usually influenced by widespread institutional support or mandates.
- *Laggards* are the last to adopt PBL and are often resistant until it becomes the standard or is required.

In addition to understanding adopter categories, it is critical to comprehend the role opinion leaders play. An opinion leader is a well-known individual (not necessarily someone in a formal leadership role) who can influence others, has credibility among their peers, is socially connected, and enjoys an informal position and status. How can we leverage the diffusion of innovations theory to ensure that all students experience PBL? Often, district leaders think the answer is to train all teachers in PBL.

However, we encourage you to think about this a little differently. Instead of organizing PBL rollout by teacher category, try organizing it by student groups, starting with the schools that seem the most ready and have the most pro-PBL opinion leaders.

Consider using this approach to be more thoughtful about how you scale PBL districtwide. By mapping each school's journey with PBL, district leaders can see who's already on board, which schools might be ready to dive in, and which schools might need a bit of a nudge. Look at each school's willingness to try new things, its influence across the district, and how many students could benefit from PBL to ensure the strategy is impactful and fair. Within schools, start with the grade levels (elementary) or subject areas (middle and high school) that house early adopter opinion leaders. If a grade level or subject area has no early adopter opinion leaders, identify early majority opinion leader teachers and provide them with incentives.

Scaling maps are a helpful tool for planning PBL rollout. They help district and school leaders assemble cohorts with a good mix of PBL experience and readiness, pairing early adopter opinion leaders with schools that might need more inspiration to get started. The idea is to create a ripple effect in which the early adopters become PBL champions, showing other teachers and schools the real impact of PBL and making it easier for them to step into new methods. At each school, identify teachers who are both excited to try new approaches and respected by their peers. These teachers become champions within their schools, guiding others and making PBL feel less intimidating. Aim for about half of all teachers in each school to have interacted with some form of PBL by the end of the first year of implementation, with the hope that others will follow their lead.

In line with Rogers's theory, this strategy leans on early adopters to be changemakers to facilitate the organic spread of PBL across the system. By focusing on high-influence adopters and building a supportive network, district leaders can help PBL become part of the everyday teaching culture (Petrokubi et al., 2020).

As you work to develop a districtwide vision for PBL, start with some of the following actions:

- *Research how PBL can accelerate student engagement and outcomes.* (You can start with the publications found at www.pblworks.org

/research.) Share critical insights with teachers and families as appropriate.
- *Ensure your districtwide outcomes/graduate profile include deeper learning outcomes.* Have conversations with key stakeholders to either create or recommit to these outcomes.
- *Consider (with key stakeholders as appropriate) what will be different* for students, their families, the community, and the teachers as a result of PBL implementation. What will learning in your district look, sound, and feel like in three to five years?
- *Form a PBL steering committee* to inspire, support, and build coherence for PBL in your district. Typically, this group comprises district leaders and staff, school site leaders, and teacher leaders. This team should be a vertical slice of the district so that every voice is represented in matters related to PBL implementation and sustainability.
- *Use a scaling map to identify a cadre of PBL champion schools* and teachers willing to lead the way with PBL.

Culture

Chapter 4 emphasizes the importance of developing a culture for PBL that reflects what you want to see and feel in schools across the district. Figure 9.3 outlines specific knowledge and structures district leaders should prioritize as they start to develop or deepen the culture supporting PBL.

You may have heard that "culture eats strategy for breakfast," a saying often attributed to Peter Drucker in change literature and made popular by Mark Fields, former president of the Ford Motor Company. The phrase captures the importance of aligning culture with strategy, because a misaligned culture can undermine even the best of plans. The PBL implementation plans we have described are critical for success, yet they aren't sufficient. Like PBL school leaders, district leaders need to develop and sustain a districtwide culture that promotes Gold Standard PBL as a vehicle for advancing excellence and equity for all students while encouraging greater collaboration and support among teachers and leaders.

Effective leaders model the way. PBL leaders at all levels can model collaboratively examining practice by redesigning internal district or community meetings to reflect learner-centered instructional approaches,

Figure 9.3 District Leader Outcome, Practices, and Implementation Structures: Culture

Outcome	Develop and sustain a districtwide culture that promotes Gold Standard PBL as a vehicle for advancing excellence and equity for all students while encouraging greater collaboration and support among teachers and leaders.
Knowledge, skills, practices, and dispositions	• Promote effective implementation of Gold Standard PBL, emphasizing how it connects with the district's core values and promotes equity. • Model and expect adults to examine their practice collaboratively and to provide and receive high-quality peer-to-peer feedback. • Engage families and community members as active participants in presentations of learning at all levels.
Structures for implementation	• Celebrate the successful implementation of Gold Standard PBL in public settings through print and social media (e.g., communication plan) to highlight risk-taking, trust, and growth among students and adults. • Redesign district meetings to reflect Gold Standard PBL and model the Effective Project Design Elements and Project Based Teaching Practices. • Organize district presentations of learning and exhibitions to highlight student success and model a culture of transparency and learning.

Copyright © 2019 Buck Institute for Education. Reprinted with permission.

such as using a driving question to frame the meeting with inquiry. PBL leaders can also use the same protocols for giving and receiving feedback that teachers use with students to revise and critique ideas or products. We have also seen leaders share their own presentations of learning with staff.

The most potent culture-building events are those that engage families and community members as active participants at all levels in district presentations of learning and exhibitions. When the district hosts these events for the community, you can feel the energy and pride of students, their teachers, families, and community members. This creates momentum and inspiration for PBL while demonstrating that the district prioritizes and values the outcomes articulated in the graduate profile enough to make them visible to all.

Here are some suggestions for developing a districtwide culture supporting PBL:

- *Ask teachers and school leaders* who are already practicing PBL to share their experiences. Invite them to a principals' meeting or board

meeting, or host an exhibition night to build interest and excitement for PBL.
- *Redesign an upcoming district meeting* using the Gold Standard PBL Essential Project Design Elements. Introduce a challenging problem or question, provide choice through mini-sessions, engage in a critique and revision protocol, or provide opportunities to reflect on both the content and process of the meeting.
- *Review existing communication channels* to determine how to share your vision and any PBL bright spots. How will you capture and share the story of your PBL journey to inspire support, build momentum, and ensure PBL becomes the way things are done in your district?

Capacity Building

Chapters 6 and 7 emphasized the importance of capacity building for PBL. District leaders are called to support school leaders, including instructional coaches and others responsible for improving teaching and assessment. Figure 9.4 outlines specific knowledge and structures district leaders should prioritize as they build or deepen their capacity for PBL leadership.

Just as school leaders are accountable for developing the capacity of their teachers to implement Gold Standard PBL, district leaders are in turn accountable for building school leaders' capacity to put the conditions in place for teachers and students to succeed. District leaders need to provide resources—in the form of both time and money—for teachers and school leaders to undergo professional development in PBL. PBL training should not be "one and done," an add-on, or an afterthought. To fully and sustainably implement PBL, district leaders should commit to a three- to five-year plan for ongoing professional learning.

One critical component of coherent PBL implementation is identifying district policies and structures that might support or inhibit it. We recommend conducting an audit using PBLWorks's Policy and Initiative Self-Assessment (Appendix E) to identify enablers and barriers. This should spark robust dialogue that district leaders can leverage to emphasize that PBL isn't just one more thing but rather an approach that builds on, aligns with, and supports other initiatives. It might also be an opportunity to abandon initiatives that no longer serve the district's vision. Most

Figure 9.4 District Leader Outcome, Practices, and Implementation Structures: Capacity Building

Outcome	Support school leaders in their work to support teachers in developing, adapting, and implementing high-quality PBL that advances and accelerates learning for all students.
Knowledge, skills, practices, and dispositions	• Identify district policies and structures that might support or inhibit the implementation of Gold Standard PBL. • Develop district-level capacity to support the implementation and sustainability of PBL at the school level. • Model change leadership strategies to support school leaders.
Structures for implementation	• Audit policies and other district initiatives to review what might facilitate or get in the way of the implementation of Gold Standard PBL. • Establish an agreed-upon set of student outcomes related to academic success, success skills, and student empowerment (i.e., a graduate profile). • Develop a theory of action or framework for PBL implementation and scaling as a vehicle for students to achieve the outcomes identified in your accomplishing graduate profile.

Copyright © 2019 Buck Institute for Education. Reprinted with permission.

districts' "plates" are already full. What might need to come off the plate to make time and space for PBL?

To develop the capacity to support the implementation and sustainability of PBL, make sure all district leaders and staff understand their leadership role as it relates to supporting schools and school leaders. Everyone from curriculum leads to technology directors to equity leads should build their knowledge and understanding of Gold Standard PBL and be equipped to connect and support PBL through the lens of their focus area. District curriculum leads should evaluate curriculum and assessment mandates to determine the degree to which they are coherent and aligned with PBL practices. For example, teachers who are expected to use a pacing guide might feel stymied when implementing PBL. District leaders need to agree to trust teachers to adjust pacing guides as needed so PBL can flourish.

In addition, district assessment leads should schedule benchmark assessments concurrently with student exhibitions to make it easier for schools to implement PBL and set an expectation for presentations of learning to take place. Some school systems pull students achieving below proficiency out of PBL experiences for extra instruction. District leaders should discourage such practices and share the expectation that *all* students will engage in at least two high-quality PBL units per year—and the leaders must support schools to ensure this happens.

District leaders are also responsible for building the PBL leadership capacity of school leaders and instructional coaches at the district and school levels. Consider how you could reallocate resources to support PBL. How might you provide incentives and additional support to schools engaged in this work? For example, you could provide an incentive to engage in PBL training by organizing and funding cohorts of PBL leadership teams from schools that seem the most ready or interested in the work. You could sponsor a PBL coaching PLC for instructional coaches or create a PBL resource hub. Or you could host summer PBL training for teachers and provide participants with financial or professional learning incentives to complete it.

Modeling change leadership strategies as a district leader not only promotes the culture the leader aspires to see in the district but also builds the capacity of school leaders. For example, forming a district PBL steering committee can inspire schools to form school-level PBL steering committees. Engaging in a policy and initiative audit at the district level encourages school leaders to do the same. As described earlier in the chapter, creating a graduate profile is an excellent opportunity for the district leader to demonstrate how to build a shared vision with their constituents. District leaders should ensure their school leaders receive the training they need to communicate the district's PBL strategy and how it aligns with the district's overall goals to their school-level community.

Consider taking the following actions to build your capacity to lead for PBL at the district level:

- *Develop cohorts of PBL champion schools* and teachers willing to lead the way with PBL.
- *Build in-house expertise* by sending your district PBL steering committee and individuals from PBL champion schools to formal training or conferences or to visit other districts and schools.
- *Engage your PBL steering committee and critical district personnel in PBL book studies* with PBLWorks's Project Based Learning Handbooks (www.pblworks.org/handbook).
- *Create PBL coaching positions* or PBL PLCs at the district level.

- *Revisit district professional learning plans* to ensure that they prioritize PBL.
- *Provide incentives* to schools and teachers to engage in PBL professional learning.

Continuous Improvement

In Chapter 8, we unpacked how school leaders can approach continuous improvement using the School PBL Evidence Framework to assess readiness, implementation, and student outcome indicators. District leaders can use the same approach to model and create the systemic alignment needed for deep and sustained implementation using the PBLWorks District PBL Evidence Framework Toolkit (Kingston & Wagner, 2021; www.pblworks.org/research-district-pbl-evidence-framework-toolkit). Figure 9.5 outlines the specific knowledge and structures district leaders should prioritize when using the toolkit to lead an ongoing process of reflection, adaptation, and growth to improve student learning outcomes using Gold Standard PBL.

The District PBL Evidence Framework Toolkit was developed in partnership with two districts, Pearl City–Waipahu Complex Area in

Figure 9.5 District Leader Outcome, Practices, and Implementation Structures: Continuous Improvement

Outcome	Lead an ongoing process of reflection, adaptation, and growth to improve student learning outcomes through the use of Gold Standard PBL.
Knowledge, skills, practices, and dispositions	• Lead the development of a District PBL Evidence Framework to measure and track progress toward graduate profile outcomes and key indicators at the school, classroom, and student levels. • Create opportunities for schools to learn about the implementation of Gold Standard PBL with and from one another.
Structures for implementation	• Develop a District PBL Evidence Framework that articulates key indicators and drives discussions about student learning and success. • Establish cohorts of schools to share dedicated time to learn with and from one another (e.g., PBL PLCs). • Conduct leadership learning walks as an integral means of collecting data, reflecting on practice, and giving constructive feedback.

Copyright © 2019 Buck Institute for Education. Reprinted with permission.

Hawai'i and Manchester School District in New Hampshire, as part of a Scaling HQPBL for Deeper Learning grant. The aim was to create a tool for district leaders to guide their district and school teams through PBL implementation. The framework includes readiness, leading indicators, and academic and success skills components (Figure 9.6). The readiness component identifies conditions that need to be in place to scale Gold Standard PBL districtwide. Leading indicators assess school leadership, teaching and learning, and the student experience. The academic and success skills component addresses how students demonstrate mastery of key outcomes through Gold Standard PBL. The skills identified in this component come from the district's graduate profile. Although following a district-level framework from the onset of your district's PBL journey would be ideal, we have worked with many districts farther along the metaphorical path who have successfully leveraged the toolkit to deepen or reignite their PBL implementation.

The short-cycle continuous improvement model introduced in Chapter 8 also applies to PBL district leaders. During the planning phase, district leaders should determine readiness for PBL, identify clear success indicators, and develop a rollout strategy with a solid communication plan. During this phase, district leaders should focus on the following questions: "Are we ready? Where are we going? How will we get there?"

During the implement and collect data phase, district leaders should assess the state of the district's PBL journey. Even if you are already well on your way, don't miss the opportunity to collect baseline data to document the story of your progress and growth over time. This step asks the following questions: "Where are we now? How are we progressing in our PBL journey?"

In the reflect phase, district leaders analyze and reflect on implementation data and note what they see as a team. We caution against jumping too quickly to the next step and instead encourage your team to notice, frame, and interpret information together to obtain more profound understanding and insights. Use protocols to build collective meaning and ensure equity of voice.

The refine phase is designed to answer the question "What might we do differently?" In this step, the focus of the conversation should turn to inferences and recommendations based on observations made during the reflect phase. Discussing inferences or judgments about the data deepens

Figure 9.6 District PBL Evidence Framework

READINESS	LEADING INDICATORS			ACADEMIC AND SUCCESS SKILLS
Are we ready?	Is our implementation on track?			Are we making progress?
	PBL School Leadership	PBL School Conditions	PBL Design & Teaching	High-Quality PBL (HQPBL) Student Experiences
District Leadership District vision inclusive of academic and success skills (and/or graduate profile) Established district leadership team responsible for districtwide PBL implementation **School Leadership** Established school leadership team responsible for schoolwide PBL implementation **Teachers** Cadre of teachers who are PBL champions or willing to lead PBL	% of principals who report that they . . . • Are confident in their ability to lead Gold Standard PBL implementation at their school *Measured by PBL Implementation Pulse Surveys (minimally quarterly)* • Have the support they need to lead the implementation of Gold Standard PBL well *Measured by PBL Implementation Pulse Surveys (minimally quarterly)* • Believe that PBL, when done well, can be used as a primary teaching method for all students, including those furthest from opportunity *Measured by PBL Implementation Pulse Surveys (minimally quarterly)*	% of schools with . . . • Instructional schedules with blocks of time for students to engage in Gold Standard PBL (equivalent of at least 75 minutes twice a week) *Measured by PBL Implementation Pulse Surveys (minimally quarterly)* • Teachers who have the collaborative planning time they need to design projects and to effectively use Gold Standard PBL Project Based Teaching Practices (at least equivalent to 6 hours/month) *Measured by PBL Implementation Pulse Surveys (minimally quarterly)*	% of teachers who report that they . . . • Understand Gold Standard PBL Essential Project Design Elements *Measured by PBL Implementation Pulse Surveys (minimally quarterly)* • Facilitate PBL using Gold Standard PBL Project Based Teaching Practices with confidence *Measured by PBL Implementation Pulse Surveys (minimally quarterly)* • Believe that Gold Standard PBL can be used as a primary teaching method for all students, including those furthest from opportunity *Measured by PBL Implementation Pulse Surveys (minimally quarterly)*	% of students, including those who are furthest from opportunity, whose teachers report engaging in . . . • At least 2 Gold Standard PBL projects each year *Measured by project tracking tool* % of teachers and/or students, including those who are furthest from opportunity, who report that students . . . • Engage in projects aligned to the HQPBL criteria *Measured by Teacher & Student HQPBL Surveys* • Engage in at least 2 student exhibitions of learning each year *Measured by PBL Implementation Pulse Surveys (minimally quarterly)*	**Academic & Success Skills** % of students, including those who are furthest from opportunity, who report or demonstrate . . . • Critical thinking • Collaboration • Communication • Creativity • Self-direction • Mastery of academic core content *Measured by success skills rubrics and study survey of success skills*

Source: From *District PBL Evidence Framework Toolkit* (p. 12), by S. Kingston and K. Wagner, 2021, Buck Institute for Education. Copyright 2021 by Buck Institute for Education. Adapted with permission.

the inquiry and adds value to the data before shifting to actionable next steps. Using a protocol allows team members to reflect individually and share thinking before collectively considering the next steps.

In addition to leveraging the District PBL Evidence Framework, we have learned that the most effective PBL implementation happens when district leadership creates opportunities for schools to learn with and from one another. Two strategies to bring this to life have proven to be game changers for districts we partner with. The first is establishing cohorts of schools and providing dedicated time for them to learn collaboratively in PBL professional learning communities. These PLCs should provide time and space for school leadership teams to learn about best practices related to PBL implementation from both outside experts and each other while offering a safe space to share bright spots and implementation challenges. School-level PBL implementation plans and indicators should be regularly updated or examined during these sessions as appropriate. Some districts schedule quarterly full-day meetings and monthly role-specific implementation conference calls for school leadership teams, while others repurpose existing meetings and support structures to focus specifically on PBL.

The second key practice is to center leadership learning walks (see p. 95) as an integral means of collecting data, reflecting on practice, and providing constructive feedback. During leadership learning walks, districts organize visits to up to three schools in one day. At each school, the hosting PBL leadership team spends about an hour framing a problem of practice related to their PBL implementation. They share evidence and perspectives related to the challenge while leaders from the other two schools and up to three district leaders listen, ask questions, and offer insights into how to address the challenge. The process is repeated at the other two schools, and the group holds a collective debrief at the end of the day. Inviting leaders to visit each other's schools and make their work visible unlocks deep thinking and new ways of approaching the work, strengthening the entire PBL ecosystem.

Here are some strategies to consider as you work toward continuous improvement of PBL implementation in your district:

- *Review the District PBL Evidence Framework Toolkit* with those directly responsible for school improvement in your district to determine congruence with and differences from your PBL implementation plans.

- *Consider current indicators and data collection methods* for your teaching and learning initiatives. Where is there alignment with your PBL implementation plans? What processes could be streamlined?
- *Invite leaders* interested or already engaged in PBL to a roundtable session to learn more about PBL bright spots and implementation barriers.

We hope you now better understand your role as a district leader in building coherence for Gold Standard PBL. Let's turn to a case study to learn how one district leader built coherence by clearly articulating her commitment to PBL and her vision for how it served and aligned with other district initiatives.

Leadership Story: Increasing Rigor and Relevance Through PBL

In the mid-2010s, the board of the San Leandro Unified School District (SLUSD) in California issued a call to action to increase rigor in SLUSD classrooms and elevate hands-on, relevant learning for the district's 9,000 students, most of whom come from economically disadvantaged communities of color. As the new deputy superintendent of the Educational Services Division, Rosanna Mucetti helped launch a strategic plan to answer that call.

After first helping the district establish essential foundational supports, including state-of-the-art technology for every classroom and curricular resources for teachers, she began the work of shifting the district to PBL, a pedagogical model and approach that she knew had the power and capacity to transform teaching and learning in the district.

This was a huge undertaking involving 13 schools, 500 teachers and staff, and 9,000 students and families. Through intensive collaboration with the board, teachers union, and school leaders, the district set a goal for every student to experience at least one high-quality PBL project every year.

The goal was ambitious. How does a leader get the school board, district leadership, school leaders, and teachers all on board and in agreement with such a big change? Ms. Mucetti's approach involved four key steps:

1. *Assess for readiness.* Interrogate the system to understand what teachers and schools need. Understand that introducing a new pedagogical approach essentially means asking teachers to change the way they do their jobs. Be sure to listen well, address their concerns, and give them the training, materials, and support they need to succeed.
2. *Clear the barriers.* As much as possible, anticipate barriers and clear them preemptively, such as by furnishing every classroom with high-quality technology tools. Identify what infrastructure the district needs to put in place to support the new pedagogy.
3. *Educate and support key people.* Recognize that board members and principals need to be able to explain the change to teachers and families. Build the courage, knowledge, and capacity of the people in these key roles to set them up for success in communicating and supporting the change.
4. *Build the right relationships.* In any collaborative endeavor, strong relationships are essential. Invest in relationships with critical stakeholders such as the teachers union. Establishing consistent, collaborative partnerships better serves students and families.

Following those steps resulted in resounding success for students. Ms. Mucetti noted:

> PBL created rigor and relevance in a way that traditional curriculum or instructional models cannot. Those initial projects led to so much more student agency and students actually engaging with topics. There's a real sense of self-empowerment because the kids can see themselves more and feel like active agents in their learning. They're working with topics that are more culturally, linguistically, and racially relevant to their world. That experience can just completely change a student's trajectory in terms of their engagement with the educational system.

The project also excited San Leandro's teachers. Under Ms. Mucetti's leadership, the district brought in excellent training and support from PBLWorks, so teachers received the resources, capacity building skills, and tools to bring about real change in their classrooms. With that high level of support, teachers enthusiastically embraced the shift to PBL, recognizing the powerful difference it made for student learning.

PBL District Leadership in Practice

To help you put your new knowledge into practice, here are some mini-trials that you can use to explore what it's like to build coherence for PBL in your district. We encourage you to try at least one thing. Afterward, record your reflections and note any new insights you acquired.

1. Review the district's vision and outcomes for students and determine how they align with deeper learning, PBL, and academic and success skills.
2. Complete PBLWorks's District Conditions Inventory (Appendix F) and determine your current reality related to PBL district leadership. You can do this individually or with a broader team of district leaders, school leaders, and teachers. Listen with empathy to other team members. Discuss their contributions and note the implications.
3. Use the PBL Readiness Checklist in Appendix G to assess your district's readiness to implement PBL. Identify one or two immediate actions you can take to advance this work.
4. Review the agenda for a past or upcoming district meeting and consider how you could redesign it to reflect and model at least one Essential Project Design Element or Project Based Teaching Practice.

Reflect

What did you try? What did you learn from your experience?

How has your view of your role as a district leader supporting PBL shifted?

What are one to three actions you can take for quick wins to create coherence in your district's vision for PBL?

Final Reflections

1. Revisit your original mental model of building coherence for PBL. How does it connect to what you have read so far? Did your mental model change? If so, in what ways? If not, why not?
2. What aspects of your district's current reality related to PBL implementation align with the District Logic Model (Figure 9.1)? How might you strengthen coherence?
3. Review the outcomes, practices, and implementation structures for vision (Figure 9.2), culture (Figure 9.3), capacity building (Figure 9.4), and continuous improvement (Figure 9.5). How would you rate yourself with regard to these outcomes? What are your strengths? Where are your opportunities to grow?
4. Revisit this chapter's leadership story. In what ways did Ms. Mucetti build coherence to strengthen her district's PBL implementation? What lessons could you apply to your setting or practice?

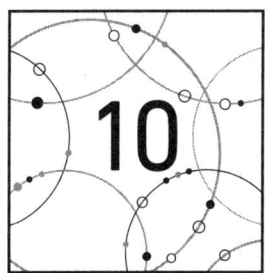

Onward to Deeper Learning

It's a journey. You can't just do it overnight. So you just do one little thing, one little nugget to get you a little closer, then add a second nugget, and another. So go slow.

—Beth Hert, principal, founding principal,
Corona Arts & Sciences Academy, Queens, New York

We started this book with our PBL leadership stories. Now, it's time to write your own story. The good news is you have already started! Engaging in the Know–Do–Reflect process throughout the book has deepened your understanding of your role as the driver or accelerator for PBL implementation. By now, you know and can demonstrate much of the knowledge and many of the skills, practices, and mindsets needed to create the conditions to grow PBL in your school or district. In essence, you have already written your introduction. As you begin to write the heart of your story, we encourage you to engage in some relentless reflection on specific themes.

Centering Equity

Revisit the PBL Equity Levers in Figure 1.3 on page 8. How might you keep this framework at the forefront of your mind as you work to create more inclusive and equitable learning experiences and outcomes for all students and adults within your school or district?

Knowledge of Students, Teachers, and Leaders

Most school leaders know from their experience with change efforts that what works for one school may not work for another. You know your learners, teachers, and community best and have the best sense of what has been done before, what will inspire, and what will be viewed as "over the top." Remember, you don't have to do it all at once. In our experience, it is often better to go slowly at first on the road to deep and sustained PBL implementation. To ensure PBL will capture students' interests, honor their strengths and identities, and meet their needs, we remind you to provide the same types of learning experiences for your teachers and leaders. For this to happen, you need to maintain an asset-based lens; prioritize relationships with students, teachers, and leaders; and be aware of how your perspective, cultural lenses, and biases can shape and hopefully strengthen your approach to PBL planning and implementation.

Cognitive Demand

To ensure that all students are engaged in intellectually challenging work, know their teachers believe in them, and have appropriate supports to advance their academic mindsets and cognitive growth, you must model and provide the same for your teachers and leaders. Thus, you need to provide varied and ongoing types and levels of training and support options and regularly remind teachers and leaders that you believe in their ability to engage in challenging and quality work with one another and their students.

At first, this may be challenging. Implementing PBL can be cognitively demanding for teachers and leaders. Even in the most supportive environments, systemic forces and balancing loops can slow down or derail well-intended and thoughtful implementation plans. Recall the discussion of creative tension in Chapter 2. Remember to hold on to your vision for PBL, rather than lowering your expectations, when you encounter the inevitable pushback, bumps, and challenges that come with most change efforts. Maintain high expectations for teachers and leaders to effectively implement PBL in their context, meet them where they are, and nudge them to the next level, much like you want your teachers to do with their students.

Literacy

One significant benefit of using Gold Standard PBL as a primary pedagogy within a school or school system is that every unit naturally incorporates literacy skills. Along with disciplinary literacy, students will strengthen reading, writing, speaking, and listening skills as they build knowledge, work with their project teams, develop prototypes, and share their learning. They will also develop information, media, and technology literacy as they find, evaluate, and use information to deepen their content knowledge and find answers to the driving questions they explore in their projects. As you plan to launch or deepen PBL implementation, consider how you can model effective literacy development strategies within the professional learning opportunities you provide for teachers and leaders. Think about it as a project with Gold Standard PBL as the "content." We encourage you to model various literacy-building strategies as you roll out PBL, with the expectation that teachers and leaders will do the same in their classrooms and schools.

Shared Power

As mentioned in Chapter 1, PBL is a learner-centered approach that can positively shift power dynamics in a classroom and, ideally, within a school. In a PBL setting, students, teachers, and leaders are all co-learners. If we want students to experience student voice, choice, agency, and interdependence in their classrooms, we must consider how to provide teachers and leaders with those same things. As you work to build a culture for and implement PBL, we remind you to take every opportunity possible to create and model structures and processes that support teacher voice, choice, agency, and interdependence. As you plan for implementation, consider how to involve teachers in co-creating a graduate profile, learning agreements for staff meetings, implementation expectations, professional learning plans, and projects. You don't have to involve everyone in every decision, but you do need to establish structures and processes to gather input and feedback, foster collaboration, and build trust. Schools where PBL thrives feature high levels of teacher ownership and buy-in, clear expectations, supportive structures, and a significant amount of teacher autonomy.

Reflect

How has your mindset about leading for PBL evolved?

List three to five takeaways from engaging with this book.

What are one or two big ideas you want to get started with to foster PBL implementation in your school or district?

Time for Action

At the beginning of this book, embarking on a PBL initiative may have seemed overwhelming to you. You probably wondered where to start, how to build excitement, and how to frame the approach with your school community. We hope things are clearer after absorbing our best practices, suggestions, and ideas to consider as you prepare to launch or deepen PBL in your school or district.

PBL is more than a checklist of things to be done. It is a mindset coupled with instructional and leadership practices that center students, teachers, and leaders as learners. Rather than viewing the suggestions outlined throughout the book as a series of linear steps, assess your educational system's current reality and vision before you decide when and how to start on your PBL journey. Take advantage of the energy from the early adopters or the creative tension found in the gap between your current reality and your vision to build your plans.

To help you simultaneously focus on the "here and now" and the "there and later," we encourage you to use the planning tools described in earlier chapters, such as the School and District PBL Evidence Frameworks offered in Chapters 8 and 9. We also want to share a couple of PBLWorks planning tools that may provide helpful guidance:

- *PBL School Implementation Planning Tool (Appendix H).* This tool, organized by the four domains of vision, culture, capacity building, and continuous improvement, synthesizes many of the ideas in the book and allows you to see them at a glance. We encourage you to use the tool as an anchor to stay on the right track.
- *PBL Action Plan Template (Appendix I).* This tool includes reflection prompts, planning resources, and a calendar to help you and your team create detailed plans as you launch your PBL implementation. We encourage you to use the PBL Action Plan Template to guide your day-to-day work.

Although we especially value these tools, we understand that schools and districts often require following plans that they already have in place. How might you center PBL in your existing plans? For example, how might PBL fit into your annual plan, accreditation action plan, technology plan, or Title I plan?

While planning for success is critical, we caution you to avoid focusing on planning more than doing. In other words, keep the emphasis on action. You don't have to have everything strategically organized before you start. Just like a project, implementing PBL at the school or district level can be "messy." We encourage you to *start*—and to leave plenty of room in your plans for inquiry, reflection, and ongoing adjustments. To that end, consider thinking about implementation just like you would think about planning a Gold Standard PBL project using the phases of the Project Path. Let's unpack how you might approach this.

First, identify initial focus areas and priorities. Next, develop a driving question. What challenging problem or question do you hope to answer with PBL? Consider the key knowledge, understanding, and skills teachers and leaders need to acquire to answer the driving question. Make sure the question is open-ended, aligned to your learning goals, and engaging and inspiring for teachers and leaders.

Once you clearly define your learning goals and the driving question, establish criteria for success. What public products can teachers and leaders create to demonstrate their answers to the driving question? Who will they share their answers and products with? Finally, start brainstorming ideas for each phase of the Project Path. Use the template in Figure 10.1 to record your plans.

Regardless of which planning tool(s) you use, remember that your plan should be a living document that you continually refine based on the needs that emerge as you implement PBL in your context. Although you should stay true to your vision, learning goals, success criteria, and expectations for implementation, we encourage you to keep your action plans relatively high-level and flexible so you can be responsive to emergent needs and insights you glean from engaging in continuous improvement processes.

You are now ready to write the next chapter of your PBL success story. Remember that every student, teacher, and leader you work with will be writing their own stories alongside you. Your work is to inspire them and create the conditions for their stories to serve as bright spots and beacons illuminating what is possible with project based learning. We can't wait to read them.

Onward to deeper learning,
Bob and Lisa

Final Final Reflections

1. What will your PBL story be?
2. Who can you lean on to bring your story to life?
3. What are you waiting for?

Figure 10.1 Project Path Action Plan

Launch Project: Entry Event and Driving Question	
How will you share your vision and spark curiosity, interest, and wonder for the PBL initiative?	
Considerations	**My Ideas**
• What is the **driving question**? (e.g., How do we ensure a successful and sustained PBL implementation?) • What kind of **entry event** will kick off implementation? (e.g., student panel, compelling video, teacher testimony, Project Slice, field trip to a PBL school) • How will you gather **need-to-know questions**? (e.g., have teachers start individual or collaborative need-to-know lists after the entry event and keep revisiting them throughout the year) • How will you build a culture for PBL?	
Build Knowledge, Understanding, and Skills to Answer the Driving Question	
How will you build student, teacher, and leader knowledge, understanding, and skills related to Gold Standard PBL?	
Considerations	**My Ideas**
• How might you leverage the diffusion of innovations theory to determine who to start with? • What PBL learning experiences and resources will you provide teachers and leaders to answer their need-to-know questions? (e.g., book study; PBL resource hub; PBL PLCs; PBL training for teachers, instructional coaches, and leaders) • How much voice and choice will teachers and leaders have to determine how they learn about PBL? • How will you ensure your school or district professional learning plan centers PBL? • When and how will you model Gold Standard PBL Project Based Teaching Practices and Essential Project Design Elements?	

Figure 10.1 Project Path Action Plan *(continued)*

Develop and Critique Products and Answers to the Driving Question		
How will students, teachers, and leaders develop and critique each other's projects?		
Considerations	**My Ideas**
• How will you create a culture of feedback? • What opportunities will teachers have to share and get feedback on their project plans and student project work? (e.g., grade-level teams will have one common planning time weekly to work on their projects, one staff meeting a quarter devoted to project tuning protocols) • How will you provide ongoing PBL coaching and support? (e.g., grade-level PLCs will become PBL-focused for the year, Online Teacher Consultancies from PBLWorks)	
Present Products and Answers to the Driving Question		
How will students, teachers, and leaders present their products and answers to the driving question?		
Considerations	**My Ideas**
• What opportunities will teachers and leaders have to share their work publicly? (e.g., staff meeting at the end of the fall semester features a teacher project exhibition, gallery walk for teachers to learn from each other) • What structures will you put in place for teachers to reflect on how their teaching practices are changing? (e.g., each teacher engages in a teacher presentation of learning once a year) • How will you capture the stories being written in classrooms and schools across the district?	

Acknowledgments

Writing this book together has been a collaborative journey of reflection, curiosity, growth, and humility. This book began to take shape thanks to the initiative and clarity of Sally Kingston, who was instrumental in helping us outline the structure and get started. Her insight gave us the confidence and momentum to move from idea to action.

We are deeply grateful to our thought partners Amanda Clark, Kelly Reseigh, and Cris Waldfogel, who not only offered critical feedback but also challenged and expanded our thinking throughout the writing process. Their voices are woven into every chapter.

A special thank you to Erin Starkey, Jason Colombino, and Rhonda Hill, whose leadership stories from their work in the field bring this work to life. Your commitment to students, teachers, and leaders grounds the ideas in this book in real-world impact.

We are fortunate to be part of a fantastic team of professional learning designers whose contributions have strengthened this work. To Rhonda Hill and Cris Waldfogel, who built the foundations of our leadership development work from the ground up, and to Dr. Laureen Adams, Kelly Reseigh, Jeannette LaFors, and Matt Keleman, past and present team collaborators—your dedication and contributions have shaped and improved this body of work immeasurably. Each of you has left a mark, and we are proud to carry this work forward with you.

And to Kristi Wagner and Sally Kingston, thank you for building the evidence frameworks and the case studies that underscore the importance and effectiveness of this approach to teaching and learning.

Many hands went into the weaving together of *Project Based Learning for All: A Leader's Guide*. We thank our colleagues, interviewees, and researchers whose perspectives and insights made our narrative richer and more complete. And we acknowledge the institutional support that allowed us to pursue this work—particularly the time, trust, and resources provided by our organization, PBLWorks, and our partners committed to equitable, deeper learning for all students.

On a personal note, we want to thank our families and friends for their patience, encouragement, and belief in us. You kept us grounded and reminded us of what matters most. And to the school leaders who were our leaders when we were teachers, you have modeled the way.

To our readers: Thank you for stepping into this work with intention and heart. May this guide help you lead with purpose, and may it catalyze meaningful change for the students, families, teachers, and leaders in your school communities.

With deep gratitude,
Bob Lenz and Lisa Mireles

Appendixes

Appendix A: Project Design Rubric.................................... 171

Appendix B: Project Based Teaching Practices Rubric 174

Appendix C: Sample Data Collection Plan 179

Appendix D: PBL Implementation Pulse Survey...................... 182

Appendix E: Policy and Initiative Self-Assessment 185

Appendix F: District Conditions Inventory........................... 189

Appendix G: District PBL Readiness Checklist 191

Appendix H: PBL School Implementation Planning Tool 193

Appendix I: PBL Action Plan Template............................... 198

Appendix J: Additional Planning Resources.......................... 201

Appendix A: Project Design Rubric

Essential Project Design Element	Beginning *This element is not yet strongly evident in this project. There are opportunities to brighten this element in future revisions of the project.*	Developing *The project includes some evidence of this Essential Project Design Element, as well as opportunities to further brighten the element in future iterations.*	Demonstrating *The project shows clear and strong evidence of this Essential Project Design Element.*
Student Learning Goals: Key Knowledge, Understanding & Success Skills	• Clear and specific student learning goals aligned to standards are not yet evident in the project. • The project does not yet explicitly target, assess, or scaffold the development of success skills.	• The project is focused on standards-derived knowledge and understanding, but it may target too few, too many, or less important goals. • Success skills are targeted, but there may be too many to be adequately taught and assessed.	• The project is focused on teaching students specific and important knowledge, understanding, and skills derived from standards and central to academic subject areas. • Success skills are explicitly targeted to be taught and assessed, such as critical thinking, collaboration, creativity, and project management.

Challenging Problem or Question	• The project is not yet focused on a central problem or question (it may be more like a unit with several tasks) or the problem or question is too easily solved or answered to justify a project.
	• The central problem or question is not framed by a driving question for the project, or the question
	  ◦ has a single or simple answer.
	  ◦ may be difficult for students to understand or connect with.
		• The project is focused on a central problem or question, but the level of challenge might be a mismatch for the intended students.
		• The driving question relates to the project but does not capture its central problem or question (it may be more like a theme).
		• The driving question meets some of the criteria for an effective driving question but lacks others.
			• The project is focused on a central problem or question at the appropriate level of challenge.
			• The project is framed by a driving question, which is
			  ◦ open-ended; there is more than one possible answer.
			  ◦ understandable and inspiring to students.
			  ◦ aligned with learning goals; to answer it, students will need to gain the intended knowledge, understanding, and skills.

(continued)

Essential Project Design Element	Beginning	Developing	Demonstrating
Sustained Inquiry	• The overall project is more like an activity or "hands-on" task rather than an extended process of inquiry. • There is no process yet for students to generate questions to guide inquiry.	• The project includes brief or intermittent opportunities for inquiry, primarily focused on information gathering. • Students generate questions, but while some might be addressed, they are not yet used to guide inquiry and do not affect the path of the project.	• Inquiry is sustained over time and academically rigorous (students pose questions, gather and interpret data, develop and evaluate solutions or build evidence for answers, and ask further questions). • Inquiry is driven by student-generated questions throughout the project.
Authenticity	• The project resembles traditional "schoolwork"; there is not yet evidence of a clear connection to a real-world context, tasks and tools, impact on the world, or connection to students' personal interests.	• The project has some authentic features, but there are opportunities to deepen connections to the real world and to students' personal interests.	• The project has an authentic context; involves real-world tasks, tools, and quality standards; makes an impact on the world; and/or speaks to students' personal concerns, interests, or identities.
Student Voice and Choice	• The project is primarily teacher-directed and does not yet include opportunities for students to express their voice and make choices affecting the content or process of the project. • (Or) Students have opportunities to work on their own but could benefit from clearer structures and guidance.	• Students are given some low-stakes opportunities to express their voice and make choices (e.g., deciding how to divide tasks within a team or which website to use for research). • Students work independently from the teacher to some extent but they could do more on their own.	• Students have opportunities to express their voice and make choices on important matters (e.g., topics to investigate, questions asked, texts and resources used, people to work with, products to be created, use of time, organization of tasks). • Students have opportunities to take significant responsibility and work as independently from the teacher as is appropriate, with guidance.
Reflection	• The project does not yet include explicit opportunities for reflection about what and how students learn or about the project's design and management.	• Students and teachers engage in brief or intermittent opportunities for reflection during the project and after its culmination.	• Students and teachers engage in thoughtful, comprehensive reflection, both during the project and after its culmination, about what and how students learn and the project's design and management.

Essential Project Design Element	Beginning	Developing	Demonstrating
Critique and Revision	• Students get some feedback about their products and work-in-progress from teachers. • Students do not yet know how or are not required to use feedback to revise and improve their work.	• Students are provided with opportunities to give and receive feedback about the quality of products and work-in-progress, but they may be unstructured or only occur once. • Students look at or listen to feedback about the quality of their work but do not have opportunities to substantially revise and improve it.	• Students are provided with regular, structured opportunities to give and receive feedback about the quality of their products and work-in-progress from peers, teachers, and if appropriate, others beyond the classroom. • Students use feedback about their work to revise and improve it.
Public Product	• The teacher is the primary audience for student work.	• Student work is made public to classmates and the teacher. • Students present products but are not asked to explain how they worked and what they learned.	• Student work is made public by presenting, displaying, or offering it to people beyond the classroom. • Students are asked to explain the reasoning behind choices they made, their inquiry process, how they worked, what they learned, etc.

Copyright © 2022 Buck Institute for Education. Reprinted with permission.

Appendix B: Project Based Teaching Practices Rubric

Project Based Teaching Practice	Beginning PBL Teacher	Developing PBL Teacher	Gold Standard PBL Teacher
Design and Plan	• Project includes some Essential Project Design Elements, but not at the highest level of the Project Design Rubric. • Plans for scaffolding and assessing student learning lack some detail; project calendar needs more detail, or is not followed. • Some resources for the project have not been anticipated or arranged in advance.	• Project includes all Essential Project Design Elements, but some are not at the highest level of the Project Design Rubric. • Plans for scaffolding and assessing student learning lack some details; project calendar allows too much or too little time, or is followed too rigidly to respond to student needs. • Most resources for the project have been anticipated and arranged in advance.	• Project includes all Essential Project Design Elements as described on the Project Design Rubric. • Plans are detailed and include scaffolding and assessing student learning and a project calendar, which remains flexible to meet student needs. • Resources for the project have been anticipated to the fullest extent possible and arranged well in advance.
Align to Standards	• Criteria for products are given but are not specifically derived from standards. • Scaffolding of student learning, critique and revision protocols, assessments, and rubrics do not refer to or support student achievement of specific standards.	• Criteria for some products are not specified clearly enough to provide evidence that students have met all targeted standards. • Scaffolding of student learning, critique and revision protocols, assessments, and rubrics do not always refer to or support student achievement of specific standards.	• Criteria for products are clearly and specifically derived from standards and allow demonstration of mastery. • Scaffolding of student learning, critique and revision protocols, assessments, and rubrics consistently refer to and support student achievement of specific standards.

Project Based Teaching Practice	Beginning PBL Teacher	Developing PBL Teacher	Gold Standard PBL Teacher
Build the Culture	• Norms are created to guide project work, but they may still feel like rules imposed and monitored by the teacher. • Students are asked for their ideas and given some choices to make, but opportunities for student voice and choice are infrequent or are only related to minor matters. • Students occasionally work independently but often look to the teacher for guidance. • Student teams are often unproductive or require frequent intervention from the teacher. • Students feel like there is a "right answer" they are supposed to give, rather than asking their own questions and arriving at their own answers; they are fearful of making mistakes. • Value is placed on "getting it done" and time is not allowed for revision of work; coverage is emphasized over quality and depth.	• Norms to guide the classroom are co-crafted with students, and students are beginning to internalize these norms. • Student voice and choice is encouraged through intentionally designed opportunities (e.g., when choosing teams, finding resources, using critique protocols, creating products). • Students work independently to some extent but look to the teacher for direction more often than necessary. • Student teams are generally productive and are learning what it means to move from cooperation to effective collaboration; the teacher occasionally has to intervene or manage their work. • Students understand there is more than one way to answer a driving question and complete the project but are still cautious about proposing and testing ideas in case they are perceived to be "wrong." • The values of critique and revision, persistence, rigorous thinking, and pride in doing high-quality work are promoted by the teacher but not yet owned by students.	• Norms to guide the classroom are co-crafted with and self-monitored by students. • Student voice and choice is regularly leveraged and ongoing, including identification of real-world issues and problems students want to address in projects. • Students usually know what they need to do with minimal direction from the teacher. • Students work collaboratively in healthy, high-functioning teams, much like an authentic work environment; the teacher rarely needs to be involved in managing teams. • Students understand there is no single "right answer" or preferred way to do the project and that it is OK to take risks, make mistakes, and learn from them. • The values of critique and revision, persistence, rigorous thinking, and pride in doing high-quality work are shared, and students hold each other accountable to them.

(continued)

Project Based Teaching Practice	Beginning PBL Teacher	Developing PBL Teacher	Gold Standard PBL Teacher
Manage Activities	• The classroom features some individual and team work time and small-group instruction, but too much time is given to whole-group instruction. • Classroom routines and norms for project work time are not clearly established; time is not used productively. • Schedules, checkpoints, and deadlines are set but are loosely followed or unrealistic; bottlenecks impede workflow. • Teams are formed using either a random process (e.g., counting off) or students are allowed to form their own teams with no formal criteria or process.	• The classroom features individual and team work time and whole-group and small-group instruction, but these structures are not well-balanced throughout the project. • Classroom routines and norms are established for project work time but are not consistently followed; productivity is variable. • Realistic schedules, checkpoints, and deadlines are set, but more flexibility is needed; bottlenecks sometimes occur. • Generally well-balanced teams are formed but without considering the specific nature of the project; students have too much voice and choice in the process or not enough.	• The classroom features an appropriate mixture of individual and team work time and whole-group and small-group instruction. • Classroom routines and norms are consistently followed during project work time to maximize productivity. • Project management tools (e.g., group calendar, contract, learning log) are used to support student self-management and independence. • Realistic schedules, checkpoints, and deadlines are set but flexible; no bottlenecks impede workflow. • Well-balanced teams are formed according to the nature of the project and student needs, with appropriate student voice and choice.
Scaffold Student Learning	• Students receive some instructional supports to access both content and resources, but many individual needs are not met. • Teacher may front-load content knowledge before the project launch, instead of waiting for "need to know" points during the project. • Students gain key success skills as a side effect of the project, but they are not taught intentionally. • Students are asked to do research or gather data but without adequate guidance; deeper questions are not generated based on information gathered.	• Most students receive instructional supports to access both content and resources, but some individual needs are not met. • Scaffolding is guided to some extent by students' questions and "need to knows" but some of it may still be front-loaded. • Key success skills are taught, but students need more opportunities to practice success skills before applying them. • Student inquiry is facilitated and scaffolded, but more is needed; teacher may over-direct the process and limit independent thinking by students.	• Each student receives necessary instructional supports to access content, skills, and resources; these supports are removed when no longer needed. • Scaffolding is guided as much as possible by students' questions and needs; teacher does not front-load too much information at the start of the project, but waits until it is needed or requested by students. • Key success skills are taught using a variety of tools and strategies; students are provided with opportunities to practice and apply them and reflect on progress. • Student inquiry is facilitated and scaffolded while allowing students to act and think as independently as possible.

Project Based Teaching Practice	Beginning PBL Teacher	Developing PBL Teacher	Gold Standard PBL Teacher
Assess Student Learning	• Student learning of subject-area standards is assessed mainly through traditional means, such as a test, rather than products; success skills are not assessed. • Team-created products are used to assess student learning, making it difficult to assess whether individual students have met standards. • Formative assessment is used occasionally but not regularly or with a variety of tools and processes. • Protocols for critique and revision are not used or are informal; feedback is superficial or not used to improve work. • Students assess their own work informally, but the teacher does not provide regular, structured opportunities to do so. • Rubrics are used to assess final products but not as a formative tool; rubrics are not derived from standards.	• Project products and other sources of evidence are used to assess subject-area standards; success skills are assessed to some extent. • Individual student learning, not just team-created products, is assessed to some extent, but teacher lacks adequate evidence of individual student mastery. • Formative assessment is used on several occasions, using a few different tools and processes. • Structured protocols for critique and revision and other formative assessments are used occasionally; students are learning how to give and use feedback. • Opportunities are provided for students to self-assess their progress but are too unstructured or infrequent. • Standards-aligned rubrics are used by the teacher to guide both formative and summative assessment.	• Project products and other sources of evidence are used to thoroughly assess subject-area standards as well as success skills. • Individual student learning, not just team-created products, is adequately assessed. • Formative assessment is used regularly and frequently, with a variety of tools and processes. • Structured protocols for critique and revision are used regularly at checkpoints; students give and receive effective feedback to inform instructional decisions and students' actions. • Regular, structured opportunities are provided for students to self-assess their progress and, when appropriate, assess peers on their performance. • Standards-aligned rubrics are used by students and the teacher throughout the project to guide both formative and summative assessment.

(continued)

Project Based Teaching Practice	Beginning PBL Teacher	Developing PBL Teacher	Gold Standard PBL Teacher
Engage and Coach	• The teacher has some knowledge of students' strengths, interests, backgrounds, and lives, but it does not significantly affect instructional decision-making. • Project goals are developed without seeking student input. • Students are willing to do the project as if it were another assignment, but the teacher does not create a sense of ownership or fuel motivation. • The driving question is presented at the project launch and student questions are generated, but they are not used to guide inquiry or product development. • Expectations for the performance of all students are not clear, too low, or too high. • There is limited relationship-building in the classroom, resulting in student needs that are not identified or addressed. • Students and the teacher informally reflect on what and how students are learning (content and process); reflection occurs mainly at the end of the project.	• The teacher has general knowledge of students' strengths, interests, backgrounds, and lives and considers it when teaching the project. • Project goals and benchmarks are set with some input from students. • Students are excited by the project and motivated to work hard by the teacher's enthusiasm and commitment to their success. • Students' questions guide inquiry to some extent, but some are answered too quickly by the teacher; students occasionally reflect on the driving question. • Appropriately high expectations for the performance of all students are set and communicated by the teacher. • Student needs for further instruction or practice, additional resources, redirection, troubleshooting, praise, encouragement, and celebration are identified through relationship-building and close observation and interaction. • Students and the teacher occasionally reflect on what and how students are learning (content and process).	• The teacher's knowledge of individual student strengths, interests, backgrounds, and lives is used to engage them in the project and inform instructional decision-making. • Students and the teacher use standards to co-define goals and benchmarks for the project (e.g., by co-constructing a rubric) in developmentally appropriate ways. • Students' enthusiasm and sense of ownership of the project is maintained by the shared nature of the work between teacher and students. • Student questions play the central role in driving the inquiry and product development process; the driving question is actively used to sustain inquiry. • Appropriately high expectations for the performance of all students are clearly established, shared, and reinforced by teacher and students. • Individual student needs are identified through close relationships built with the teacher; needs are met not only by the teacher but by students themselves or other students, acting independently. • Students and the teacher reflect regularly and formally throughout the project on what and how students are learning (content and process); they specifically note and celebrate gains and accomplishments.

Copyright © 2019 Buck Institute for Education. Reprinted with permission.

Appendix C: Sample Data Collection Plan

SCHOOL YEAR: 2023–24

Measure	Data collection tool	From whom?	When?				Analysis plan	Who is responsible?
PBL School Leadership								
Percentage of leadership team members who report that they are confident in their ability to lead Gold Standard PBL implementation at their school	PBL Implementation Pulse Survey	All PBL Leadership Team members	Oct. 10–24	Jan. 15–20	April 1–15	June 1–15	Means and frequency counts, overall and by school	J. Smith, Strategic Leadership Team (SLT)
Percentage of leadership team members who articulate that they believe PBL, when done well, is an effective instructional method for all students, including Black and Brown students								
Percentage of leadership team members who report that they have the support they need to lead the implementation of Gold Standard PBL well								
PBL Design and Teaching								
Percentage of teachers who report that they understand the Gold Standard PBL Essential Project Design Elements	PBL Implementation Pulse Survey	All teachers	Oct. 10–24	Jan. 15–20	April 1–15	June 1–15	Means and frequency counts, overall and by school	J. Smith, SLT
Percentage of teachers who report that they facilitate PBL using Gold Standard PBL Project Based Teaching Practices with confidence								
Percentage of teachers who articulate that they believe PBL, when done well, is an effective instructional method for all students, including Black and Brown students								

	PBL School Conditions					
Percentage of grade levels/departments with instructional schedules that include blocks of time for students to engage in Gold Standard PBL (equivalent of at least 75 minutes twice a week)	Document review: instructional schedules		Sep.		Feb.	Met/Not Met, with recommendations if applicable	PBL SLT, led by J. Smith
Percentage of grade levels/departments in which teachers have the collaborative planning time they need to design projects and effectively use Gold Standard PBL Project Based Teaching Practices (equivalent of at least six hours per month)	Document review: school annual professional development (PD) plan, PD team minutes, PBL Implementation Pulse Survey	All teachers		Oct.		April	
Percentage of teachers who report engaging in at least 18 hours of PBL coaching and support	PBL Implementation Pulse Survey		Oct. 10–14	Jan. 15–20	April 1–15	June 1–15	Average coaching hours experience, disaggregated by grade level/department or other identified criteria
	Student PBL Experiences						
Percentage of students, including those who are Black and Brown, whose teachers report engaging in at least two Gold Standard PBL projects each year	Project tracking tool	All grade levels (see focus areas by quarter)	Oct. 10–24 focus: grades 2, 4	Jan. 15–20, focus: grades 3, 5	April 1–15, focus: grades K, 1		Means and frequency counts, overall and by school, grade level, and/or content area	School PBL leaders, with support from J. Smith
Percentage of teachers and/or students, including Black and Brown students, who report that students engage in projects aligned to the HQPBL criteria	Teacher and/or Student HQPBL Survey					June 1–15	Means and frequency counts, overall and by criteria, school
Percentage of teachers and/or students, including Black and Brown students, who report that students engage in at least two student exhibitions or presentations of learning each year	PBL Implementation Pulse Survey	All teachers	Oct. 10–24	Jan. 15–20	April 1–15		Means and frequency counts, overall and by school

Copyright © 2021 Buck Institute for Education. Reprinted with permission.

Appendix D: PBL Implementation Pulse Survey

Thank you in advance for completing this brief survey about your experiences implementing project based learning (PBL) in your school. We are collecting data from all instructional staff across the district to identify areas of strength and ways to support PBL implementation in the district. Please check all answers that apply.

1. Your grade level and/or department: _____

2. Did you participate in PBL professional learning in the last quarter?
   ❏ Yes ❏ No

3. What is your current role?
   ❏ Classroom teacher ❏ Instructional specialist
   ❏ PBL Leadership Team member ❏ Other

4. Rate your response to the following statement: I have the support I need to lead the implementation of Gold Standard PBL well in my school.
   ❏ Strongly agree ❏ Agree ❏ Disagree ❏ Strongly disagree

5. How frequently do you have collaboration time to work on projects?
   ❏ Daily ❏ Every quarter
   ❏ Weekly ❏ Annually
   ❏ Every other week ❏ Never
   ❏ Monthly ❏ Not applicable to my role
   ❏ Every other month

6. Have you ever engaged in PBL coaching or support?
   - ❏ Yes, 1–2 hours
   - ❏ Yes, 2–4 hours
   - ❏ Yes, 4–8 hours
   - ❏ Yes, 8+ hours
   - ❏ I have not engaged in PBL coaching
   - ❏ Not applicable to my role

7. Tell us more about how that coaching or support enhanced your PBL implementation.

   _____

   _____

   _____

8. Explain what additional resources you need, if any, to facilitate PBL well.

   _____

   _____

   _____

9. In the last three months, have you facilitated a project with students?
   - ❏ Yes ❏ No ❏ Not applicable to my position

10. Indicate your level of confidence using the Gold Standard PBL Project Based Teaching Practices:

	I am confident.	I am somewhat confident.	I am not confident.
Design and plan a project	❏	❏	❏
Align to standards	❏	❏	❏
Build the culture	❏	❏	❏
Manage activities	❏	❏	❏
Scaffold student learning	❏	❏	❏
Assess student learning	❏	❏	❏
Engage and coach	❏	❏	❏

11. Did the students participate in an exhibition or presentation of learning?
    - ❏ Yes, one ❏ Yes, two or more ❏ No

12. Tell us more about your responses.

    _____

    _____

    _____

13. Indicate your current understanding of the Gold Standard PBL Essential Project Design Elements:

	I can do this independently.	I am learning and need more practice/support.	I do not understand.
Challenging problem or question	❏	❏	❏
Sustained inquiry	❏	❏	❏
Authenticity	❏	❏	❏
Student voice and choice	❏	❏	❏
Reflection	❏	❏	❏
Critique and revision	❏	❏	❏
Public product	❏	❏	❏

14. Tell us more about your responses.

_____

_____

_____

15. To what extent do you agree with the following statements?

	Strongly agree	Agree	Disagree	Strongly disagree
I understand the Gold Standard PBL Essential Project Design Elements.	❏	❏	❏	❏
I regularly use the Gold Standard PBL Project Based Teaching Practices.	❏	❏	❏	❏
PBL can be used as a primary teaching method for *all* students.	❏	❏	❏	❏
I am confident in my ability to implement PBL with students in my classroom, school, or district.	❏	❏	❏	❏

Copyright © 2021 Buck Institute for Education. Reprinted with permission.

Appendix E: Policy and Initiative Self-Assessment

Use this tool to guide a review of past and current initiatives to have a clear, shared picture of the successes, challenges, and resource commitments of existing mandates.

Step 1

Using the table below, list three to five highest priority district-level initiatives, including as much information as you can for each.

Name of Initiative + Mandated (yes/no)	Leadership of Initiative (name of leader/ key team who "owns" the work)	Target Population (who the initiative is meant to serve)	Financial Commitment (annual or total funding; funding source)	Initiative Start/ End Dates	Does the Initiative Align with District Priorities and Strategic Plan? (yes/ no/not sure)	Expected Outcomes (indicate any articulated measures)	Successful? (yes/no/not sure yet)

Step 2

Discuss each initiative using the following questions to guide the discussion:

- Given the definition of success for the initiative, was it successful? If yes, what made it so? If not, why not?
- Does the initiative align with the district's overall strategic priorities? If yes, how is or was that alignment communicated to all stakeholders? If not, discuss why not.
- Is project based learning one of the initiatives? If yes, how will you leverage the successes of other initiative rollouts to ensure commensurate success? If not, how will you communicate to all stakeholders that project based learning isn't "just one more thing"?

Discussion Notes:

Step 3

Brainstorm a list of policies that already support the implementation of PBL. Identify (using a star or highlight) any that might need to be revisited to remove PBL implementation barriers (e.g., policies related to the mandated use of specific instructional materials, pacing guides, schedules, common planning time, guest speakers, field trips). Are there any new policies you might want to introduce to support PBL? Any other anticipated barriers?

Policies that support PBL	Policies that might be a barrier to PBL	New policies we may need	Additional anticipated PBL implementation barriers	Action steps to address anticipated barriers

Step 4

Identify any new insights and potential next steps.

What new insight did you gain from conducting the self-assessment?	What are your next steps?

Appendix F: District Conditions Inventory

Use this inventory to assess the infrastructure and other district conditions necessary for implementing Gold Standard PBL effectively.

DIMENSION: VISION				
	1 Not True	2 More Untrue Than True	3 More True Than Untrue	4 True
Our district has an agreed-upon set of student outcomes related to academic success, success skills, and student empowerment (e.g., a graduate profile).				
Our district articulates a vision for how Gold Standard PBL serves and aligns with other district initiatives.				
Our district has made a public commitment that every student will engage in at least two high-quality PBL experiences every year.				
Our district has an effective implementation strategy for scaling PBL districtwide.				

DIMENSION: CULTURE				
	1 Not True	2 More Untrue Than True	3 More True Than Untrue	4 True
Our district organizes presentations of learning and exhibitions to model a culture of transparency and learning.				
Our district publicly communicates to all stakeholders the current reality of Gold Standard PBL implementation.				
Our district celebrates the successful implementation of Gold Standard PBL in public settings through print and social media.				
Our district meeting agendas incorporate Gold Standard PBL design elements.				
DIMENSION: CAPACITY BUILDING				
	1 Not True	2 More Untrue Than True	3 More True Than Untrue	4 True
Our policies and district initiatives have been audited to identify both supports for and barriers to Gold Standard PBL implementation.				
Our district allows schools the flexibility to adjust curriculum and pacing guides, teaching and assessment strategies, and financial resources to ensure robust Gold Standard PBL implementation.				
DIMENSION: CONTINUOUS IMPROVEMENT				
	1 Not True	2 More Untrue Than True	3 More True Than Untrue	4 True
Our district has an evidence framework that measures the impact of Gold Standard PBL on student learning and success.				
Learning walks are an integral part of collecting data, reflecting on practice, and giving constructive feedback.				
Our district has a system for organizing PBL cohorts to learn with and from one another.				

Copyright © 2023 Buck Institute for Education. Reprinted with permission.

Appendix G: District PBL Readiness Checklist

Review the following criteria and assess your readiness to move along your PBL journey.

❏ DISTRICT VISION FOR DEEPER LEARNING

District vision inclusive of deeper learning outcomes (and/or graduate profile)

- Our district has an agreed-upon set of student outcomes related to academic outcomes, success skills, and student empowerment.
- Our district has an articulated vision for how Gold Standard PBL aligns with other district initiatives.

❏ DISTRICT LEADERSHIP PBL IMPLEMENTATION TEAM

Established district PBL implementation team responsible for districtwide PBL implementation

Number of participants: 3–5

Team assets:

- PBL championship
- Successful experience planning and implementing complex projects
- Implementation expertise and leadership
- Implementation decision-making
- Strong instructional leadership

❏ SCHOOL LEADERSHIP PBL IMPLEMENTATION TEAMS

Established school PBL implementation teams responsible for school-wide PBL implementation

Number of participants: 3–5

Team assets:

- PBL championship
- Successful experience planning and implementing complex projects
- Person responsible for leading PBL implementation schoolwide
- Implementation decision-making
- Strong instructional leadership

❏ TEACHERS READY TO IMPLEMENT PBL

Cadre of teacher leaders who are PBL champions or willing to lead PBL implementation

Copyright © 2023 Buck Institute for Education. Reprinted with permission.

Appendix H: PBL School Implementation Planning Tool

Embarking on a project based learning initiative may seem overwhelming. Where do you start? How do you build excitement? How do you even explain PBL? There is a temptation to follow a "recipe" for success, but most school leaders know from their experience with school change efforts that what works for one school or teacher may not work for another. PBL implementation is not a checklist of things to be done but a mindset coupled with instructional and leadership practices that center the learners.

We have compiled a list of suggestions and ideas aligned with the PBLWorks Leadership Continuum and the School Conditions Inventory to help you organize your PBL implementation around typical initial milestones. You don't need to do everything on the list. You also don't need to do it all at once or in the order suggested. Instead, review the list and decide what makes the most sense in your context.

	Lay the Groundwork		
Complete?	**Considerations**	**By when?**	**Who will lead?**
	Host a project experience such as a Project Slice so students, teachers, and other stakeholders can experience PBL from a student's perspective.		
	Establish and train a PBL steering committee or leadership cadre responsible for schoolwide PBL implementation.		
	Poll teachers to determine how willing they are to adopt PBL. Use the results to create a scaling plan to train teachers over time in a thoughtful, strategic way.		
	Develop and train a cadre of teachers who champion PBL who are willing to help lead PBL implementation and create proof points.		
	Visit a nearby PBL school to learn about its successes and challenges. Discuss the takeaways and implications with your PBL leadership team and champions.		
	Build empathy and better understand your current reality by scheduling a PBL classroom walkthrough or engaging in a student shadowing protocol.		
	Review the School Conditions Inventory (Figure 5.1) with your PBL leadership team to identify gaps and opportunities. What can you address now? What might be addressed later? Revisit the inventory at least quarterly.		
	Consider how PBL builds on prior initiatives and connects to current ones. Most schools' "plates" are already very full. What is coming off your school's plate to make time and space for PBL?		
	Set the Vision: Paint the Picture		
Complete?	**Considerations**	**By when?**	**Who will lead?**
	Solidify and articulate your commitment to Gold Standard PBL and deeper learning outcomes.		
	Ensure your schoolwide outcomes and graduate profile include deeper learning competencies. Have conversations with key stakeholders to either create or recommit to these competencies.		
	In collaboration with your students, teachers, and other vital stakeholders, revisit your school mission and vision to ensure that PBL and deeper learning are reflected.		
	Engage students, teachers, and community members in sustained dialogue about how PBL and deeper learning align with the school vision, support all students to learn at high levels, and serve to diminish achievement and opportunity gaps.		

Set the Vision: Paint the Picture			
Complete?	Considerations	By when?	Who will lead?
	Clearly and regularly communicate your expectation to all stakeholders that all students will engage in at least two HQPBL experiences a year. Communications can include newsletters, conversations, meetings, videos, and your school website.		
	Create an action plan that includes the initial steps you will take to increase the frequency and deepen the quality of PBL experiences for students in your school. Revisit this plan monthly or quarterly. Share the plan with stakeholders.		
Build the Culture: Create a "Why" and Excitement for PBL			
Complete?	Considerations	By when?	Who will lead?
	Leverage the efforts of teachers who are already engaging with PBL by having them and their students share their experiences in various ways, such as at staff meetings or via video or newsletter write-ups.		
	Engage leaders and staff in trust-building exercises before facilitating, creating, and using shared agreements and core values that promote risk-taking, trust, and growth among students and adults. These exercises should happen at the staff level first so that grade-level and subject teams and teachers can lead the process at the classroom level.		
	Co-create shared agreements and expectations for implementing PBL. For example, you might work with your PBL champions and PBL leadership team to do the following: • Decide when/how students will experience projects—all teachers, all grades, all subjects; some teachers, some grades, some subjects? • Decide how often (at least twice a year) you will provide opportunities for teachers and students to share and celebrate their project work via exhibitions or presentations of learning.		
	Model discussion protocols and structures that provide safe spaces and equity of voice for teachers to give one another feedback on practice and the quality of the projects they are implementing.		
	Ask your teachers for feedback on your work and get in the habit of thanking them. Be sure to model kind, specific, and helpful feedback.		

Build the Culture: Create a "Why" and Excitement for PBL			
Complete?	Considerations	By when?	Who will lead?
	Regularly recognize and celebrate teachers and students for achieving deeper learning outcomes, especially work that contributes to advancing equity in student outcomes.		
	Encourage teachers to have visual artifacts such as project walls visible in their classrooms.		
	Plan exhibitions or presentations of learning for teachers and students to share and celebrate their project work.		
	Engage families and community members as active participants in presentations of learning at all levels.		
Build Capacity: Train and Connect Practitioners			
Complete?	Considerations	By when?	Who will lead?
	Ensure your school's professional development plan comprehensively and seamlessly integrates professional learning focused on Gold Standard PBL.		
	Lead the design and facilitation of powerful adult learning experiences related to Gold Standard PBL by ensuring staff meetings and other learning opportunities model the Essential Project Design Elements and Project Based Teaching Practices.		
	Provide explicit guidance to teachers on adjusting the pace of the curriculum to ensure the regular use of Gold Standard PBL teaching practices and deeper learning for students.		
	Ensure teachers have adequate time (at least 6 hours a month) for project development, troubleshooting, and reflection on project successes and challenges.		
	Ensure that school leadership team members, instructional coaches, and other teacher leaders are engaged in formal professional learning opportunities or coaching to develop the knowledge and skills to lead Gold Standard PBL and deeper learning based on individual needs.		
	Ensure teachers can access individualized coaching or feedback to support Gold Standard PBL and deeper learning.		
	Support teachers in learning to use performance assessments that allow students to show what they know and can do throughout a project. Make sure to monitor and support continued use.		
	Monitor and support using standards-aligned rubrics as a grading practice for projects.		

	Build a Continuous Improvement System for PBL: Monitor Implementation and Remove Barriers		
Complete?	**Considerations**	**By when?**	**Who will lead?**
	Identify priority academic and success skills to track over time. What related data do you already collect?		
	Identify a set of readiness, implementation, and student outcome indicators using the School Evidence Framework as your guide.		
	Review your current data collection plan and compare it to a Sample Data Collection Plan (Appendix C). If you don't have a data collection plan, adapt the sample to suit your needs.		
	As a PBL leadership team, with the support of your PBL champions or staff, collect and analyze evidence to track and improve progress on implementation and student outcome indicators • Regularly review a project tracker to determine evidence of teacher usage of PBL. • Regularly examine and reflect on student work for evidence of priority academic and success skills. • Regularly administer and reflect on results of the PBL Implementation Pulse Survey (Appendix D). • Regularly administer and reflect on the results of the HQPBL Teacher Survey. • Regularly administer and reflect on the results of the HQPBL Student Survey. • Regularly engage in and reflect on PBL classroom walkthroughs or PBL leadership learning walks to gather anecdotal data.	_____ _____ _____ _____ _____ _____	
	Design and lead continuous improvement cycles focused on the rate and effectiveness of implementing Gold Standard PBL. Make sure to plan, implement and collect data, reflect, and refine.		
	Regularly share successes that emerge from data collection efforts.		

Copyright © 2021 Buck Institute for Education. Reprinted with permission.

Appendix I: PBL Action Plan Template

Step 1: Reflect on what you learned about leading for PBL implementation from reading *Project Based Learning for All: A Leader's Guide*. Write down three to five big takeaways below:

Step 2: Think strategically about how you will work with key stakeholders (especially teachers) to launch or deepen schoolwide PBL implementation. What is the best way to work toward or strengthen Gold Standard PBL in your educational context? How can you build on what has already been done? How might you build coherence with existing initiatives? Jot down your big ideas:

Step 3: Review the additional planning resources in Appendix J.

Appendixes 199

Step 4: Create an action plan that includes three to five specific actions you will take in the next three months to increase the frequency and deepen the quality of PBL experiences for students in your school. Use the calendar below (or your own) to plan how the learning and structures will be sequenced and scheduled to support your school's long-term vision for PBL and ensure that *all* students experience high-quality project based learning. Make sure to include a **communication plan** as one of your steps. Add more columns as needed.

Aspiration Statement:			
	Action #1	**Action #2**	**Action #3**
What? • What are you doing? • What actions will you take? • How will these actions close gaps in both PBL access and PBL practice?			*Create a communication plan.*
Who? • Who will the target of the action be? • Who at my school will lead this? • Who else will provide support?			
When? • What is the implementation time frame? • What does the timeline look like? • (You can use the calendar below or your own calendar to map it out)			
How? • How will this be communicated? How does it fit into our larger communication about the vision and expectations around PBL?			
Indicators of Success • How will we know if our actions have the intended impact? • What evidence will we collect? • How will we monitor implementation efforts? *(E.g., % of teachers trained in PBL 101; % of teachers who report they understand Essential Project Design Elements; % of teachers who implement a project within 3 months; cadre of teachers who are PBL champions or willing to lead PBL)*			

Month:			
Week 1	**Week 2**	**Week 3**	**Week 4**

Month:			
Week 1	**Week 2**	**Week 3**	**Week 4**

Month:			
Week 1	**Week 2**	**Week 3**	**Week 4**

Appendix J: Additional Planning Resources

Adopter Category Chart

Where do the teachers in my school stand with project based learning?

People fall into a variety of categories when it comes to their willingness to adopt new technologies, strategies, and techniques. Read through the five categories and their characteristics below. Then complete the Adopter Category Chart by adding teachers' names in the column that best describes where they stand with PBL.

- **Innovators**—"I'm already doing it. I'll do it, no questions asked."
  - Are willing to innovate
  - Bring innovation in from outside the organization
  - Network outside the organization
  - Are venturesome
  - Use the future as their point of reference
- **Early Adopters**—"It sounds like a good idea—why not? I would consider it."
  - Are sought out by others for their advice
  - Are integrated into the system
  - Show the greatest degree of opinion leadership
  - Have the respect of their peers
  - Are successful

- **Early Majority**—"I want to research it before I do it."
    - Interact well and often with others in the system
    - Are seldom opinion leaders
    - Deliberate about adopting innovations
    - Wait until they are sure they will get value out of it
    - Are generally risk-averse
- **Late Majority**—"I'm willing to do it if I have to."
    - Are skeptical about innovations and outcomes
    - Are price-sensitive
    - Need peer pressure for motivation
- **Laggards**—"It's not on my radar. Why would I consider it?"
    - Are traditional
    - Show more skepticism than other groups
    - Have limited resources
    - Lack awareness
    - Demonstrate no opinion leadership
    - Use the past as their point of reference

Adopter Category Chart				
Innovators	Early Adopters	Early Majority	Late Majority	Laggards

Who are the opinion leaders in my school?

An opinion leader is a well-known individual who can influence public opinion on certain subject matters. Being an opinion leader is not based on a person's formal position in the school. Instead, it derives from the ability to influence others, credibility among peers, social connection, and informal position and status.

Add a star next to the names of opinion leaders in the Adopter Category Chart (regardless of which column they're in).

PBL Adoption Curve

What is my school's PBL Adoption Curve?

Determine your school's PBL Adoption Curve using data from the Adopter Category Chart. On the y axis is the number of teachers, and on the x axis add the number/percentage of teachers in each adopter category. Add stars in each adopter category for the opinion leaders.

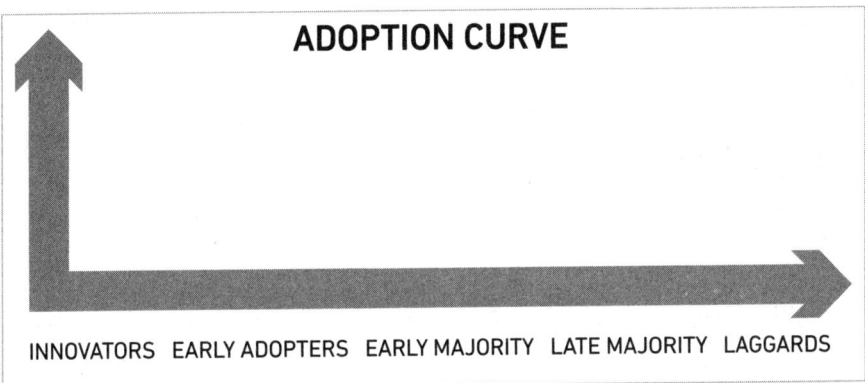

Review your PBL Adoption Curve to determine which teachers you will train first, then highlight their names in the Adopter Category Chart. You will want to select a healthy mix of Early Adopters and the Early Majority.

Characteristics of Innovation

Adoption rates are influenced by the characteristics of the specific innovation (in this case, PBL). Adopters will consider relative advantage, compatibility, complexity, trialability, and observability when making their decision on whether to adopt a specific innovation. Understanding the characteristics of innovation can help you determine quick wins to improve adoption rates.

Review the explanation of each characteristic below, then reflect on ways you might address these characteristics with teachers to mitigate any barriers to implementation. Review the Quick Win Strategies in the next section for specific actions related to the various characteristics of innovation.

Relative Advantage

An observation of the advantages and benefits of adopting a specific innovation.

- Innovation is an improvement over something already existing, so potential adopters must first calculate the relative strengths of the innovation over the status quo.
  - What is the advantage of PBL over traditional teaching and learning?
  - What improvements does PBL promise?
- Individuals who recognize an advantage to PBL will be more likely to adopt it.

Compatibility

The extent to which an innovation is compatible with existing values, norms, and goals.

- How well does PBL fit into a person's needs, usage patterns, and/or current value system?
- How consistent is PBL with how the school or district does business?
- What other initiatives, if any, can or does PBL integrate with?
- What are school leaders already doing that PBL can build on?

Complexity

The level of difficulty that potential users encounter with an innovation.

- How complex is PBL to learn?
- How complex is PBL to facilitate?
- How complex is PBL to implement schoolwide?

Trialability

The ability to try out the innovation by taking a "test drive."

- How easily can PBL be tested in the school?
- To what extent does the school or district culture promote risk-taking?
- To what extent is PBL being tested in the school? In which classrooms?

Observability

The visibility of the benefits of an innovation. The more obvious the advantages, the faster an innovation will be adopted.

- How visible are the results of PBL to school leaders?
- How visible are the results and benefits of PBL to teachers?
- How visible are the results and benefits of PBL to parents and other community stakeholders?
- Which teachers/classrooms are engaging with PBL?

Quick Win Strategies for Scaling PBL

Review the chart below for some potential Quick Win Strategies to address the various characteristics of innovation. Highlight which quick wins you will add to your action plan.

Quick Win Strategy	Relative advantage	Compatibility	Complexity	Trialability	Observability
Frame and target messaging about the benefits of PBL.	▲				
Frame and target messaging about how PBL aligns with school goals, strategies, and existing initiatives.		▲			
Share stories of teacher/school success using PBL ("bright spots").	▲				▲
Create a district graduate profile incorporating deeper learning competencies.		▲			
Share results of a recent PBL literature review.	▲				
Attend PBL exhibitions at nearby PBL schools.					▲
Make and share videos of diverse learners in the school engaged in PBL.	▲				▲
Create a plan for district educators and community members to visit schools where PBL is being done well.					▲
Create a culture that promotes risk-taking and trying out PBL.				▲	
Create tools, resources, and support to reduce the complexity of PBL.			▲		
Develop a strategy to encourage testing out PBL (e.g., small innovation grants). Allow for and encourage "mini-projects" as a way to start.				▲	

PBL Communication Plan

When communicating your vision and plan for PBL, it's essential to keep a few things in mind:

- Make sure your "why" for PBL is central to your communication. Can you articulate your "why" in one sentence? We recommend the 27–9–3 rule: Use no more than 27 words with 3 big ideas that can be shared in 9 seconds.
- Focus on no more than **three big ideas:**
  - The vision for PBL and the "why" as it relates to students
  - How PBL aligns with or builds on other school initiatives in service of your school goals
  - The nuts and bolts of implementation expectations—a high-level timeline.
- Keep it simple and to the point.
- Get feedback on your plan from colleagues and refine your plan based on that feedback.

Copyright © 2019 Buck Institute for Education. Reprinted with permission.

References

Baines, A. M., De Vivo, K., Warner, N., DeBarger, A., Udall, D., Zuckerbrod, N., & Felsen, K. (2021). *Why social and emotional learning is essential to project-based learning.* Lucas Education Research. https://www.lucasedresearch.org/docs/sel/

Bellanca, J. A. (Ed.). (2016). *Connecting the dots: Teacher effectiveness and deeper professional learning.* Solution Tree Press.

Berger, R., Rugen, L., & Woodfin, L. (2014). *Leaders of their own learning: Transforming schools through student-engaged assessment.* Jossey-Bass.

Berglund, T., Clay, I., Giglio, K., Gittens, A. D., Kaufman, J. H., Kennedy, K. E., Opfer, V. D., Pauketat, R., Polikoff, M., Schweig, J., Silver, D., Wang, E. L., & Woo A. (2024). *Coherence in K–12 instructional systems: What we know and where we can go.* RAND. https://www.rand.org/pubs/research_briefs/RBA279-1.html

Bird, K. (2018). *Generative scribing: A social art of the 21st century.* Pi Press.

Bitter, C., Taylor, J., Zeiser, K. L., & Rickles, J. (2014). *Providing opportunities for deeper learning* (Report 2). American Institutes for Research. https://www.air.org/sites/default/files/downloads/report/Report%202%20Providing%20Opportunities%20for%20Deeper%20Learning%209-23-14.pdf

Boss, S., & Larmer, J. (2018). *Project based teaching: How to create rigorous and engaging learning experiences.* ASCD; Buck Institute for Education.

Brandt, W. C. (2024). *Measuring student success skills: A review of the literature on student agency.* National Center for the Improvement of Educational Assessment. https://www.nciea.org/wp-content/uploads/2025/01/Student-Agency-Report-Final.pdf

Brown, C., & Mednick, A. (2012). *Quality performance assessment: A guide for schools and districts.* Center for Collaborative Education.

Brown, D. J. (2014). *The boys in the boat: Nine Americans and their epic quest for gold at the 1936 Berlin Olympics.* Penguin Publishing Group.

Buck Institute for Education. (n.d.). *PBLWorks: What is PBL?* https://www.pblworks.org/what-is-pbl

Carnegie Foundation. (2024, November 20). *Unlocking student potential: Aurora Institute's Virgel Hammonds on the power of competency-based education.* Carnegie Foundation for the Advancement of Teaching. https://www.carnegiefoundation.org/blog/unlocking-student-potential-aurora-institutes-virgel-hammonds-on-the-power-of-competency-based-education/

Cheema, A., & Bagchi, R. (2011). The effect of goal visualization on goal pursuit: Implications for consumers and managers. *Journal of Marketing, 75*(2), 109–123. https://doi.org/10.1509/jm.75.2.109

Condliffe, B., Quint, J., Visher, M. G., Bangser, M., Drohojowska, S., Saco, L., & Nelson, E. (2017, October). *Project-based learning: A literature review.* MDRC. https://www.mdrc.org/sites/default/files/Project-Based_Learning-LitRev_Final.pdf

Costa, A. L., Garmston, R. J., Hayes, C., & Ellison, J. (2016). *Cognitive coaching: Developing self-directed leaders and learners.* Rowman & Littlefield.

Costa, A. L., Garmston, R. J., & Zimmerman, D. P. (2014). *Cognitive capital: Investing in teacher quality.* Teachers College Press.

Costa, A. L., & Kallick, B. (Eds.). (1995). *Assessment in the learning organization: Shifting the paradigm*. ASCD.

Craik, K. J. W. (1943). *The nature of explanation*. Cambridge University Press.

Crisp, S. (2017, October 30). *A day in the life of a principal | U.S.* U.S. Department of Education. http://web.archive.org/web/20240724193321/https://www.ed.gov/content/day-life-principal

Davis, W. (2009). *The wayfinders: Why ancient wisdom matters in the modern world*. House of Anansi Press.

Delpit, L., & Dowdy, J. K. (Eds.). (2008). *The skin that we speak: Thoughts on language and culture in the classroom* (New ed.). New Press.

Duke, N. K., Halvorsen, A.-L., Strachan, S. L., Kim, J., & Konstantopoulos, S. (2021). Putting PjBL to the test: The impact of project-based learning on second graders' social studies and literacy learning and motivation in low-SES school settings. *American Educational Research Journal, 58*(1), 160–200. https://doi.org/10.3102/0002831220929638

Dweck, C. S., & Leggett, E. L. (1988). A social-cognitive approach to motivation and personality. *Psychological Review, 95*(2), 256–273. https://doi.org/10.1037/0033-295X.95.2.256

Envision Education. (n.d.). Our students. https://envisionschools.org/our-students/

Fester, J. (2022, June 17). *5 ways leaders can support Gold Standard PBL*. PBLWorks. https://www.pblworks.org/blog/5-ways-leaders-can-support-gold-standard-pbl

Field, S. (2021, March 11). *4 equity levers in project based learning*. PBLWorks. https://www.pblworks.org/blog/4-equity-levers-project-based-learning

Fixsen, D. (2016, June 22). *NIRN: Formula for success*. University of North Carolina Chapel Hill. https://hml.fpg.unc.edu/Play/4387

Fixsen, D. L., Naoom, S. F., Blase, K. A., Friedman, R. M., & Wallace, F. (2005). *Implementation research: A synthesis of the literature*. (FMHI Publication #231). University of South Florida, Louis de la Parte Florida Mental Health Institute, The National Implementation Research Network. https://nirn.fpg.unc.edu/wp-content/uploads/NIRN-MonographFull-01-2005.pdf

Friedlaender, D., Burns, D., Lewis-Charp, H., Cook-Harvey, C. M., & Darling-Hammond, L. (2014). *Student-centered schools: Closing the opportunity gap*. Stanford Center for Opportunity Policy in Education. https://learningpolicyinstitute.org/sites/default/files/2024-03/Student_Centered_Learning_SCOPE_CROSSCASE_RESEARCH_BRIEF.pdf

Fullan, M. (2020). *Leading in a culture of change* (2nd ed.). Jossey-Bass.

Gonser, S. (2021, September 20). *Ron Berger on the power of "beautiful work."* Edutopia. https://www.edutopia.org/article/ron-berger-power-beautiful-work/

Gottfredson, R., & Reina, C. (2020, January 17). *To be a great leader, you need the right mindset*. Harvard Business Review. https://hbr.org/2020/01/to-be-a-great-leader-you-need-the-right-mindset

Grissom, J. A., Egalite, A. J., & Lindsay, C. A. (2021). *How principals affect students and schools: A systematic synthesis of two decades of research*. The Wallace Foundation. https://wallacefoundation.org/sites/default/files/2023-09/How-Principals-Affect-Students-and-Schools.pdf

Hammond, Z. (2015). *Culturally responsive teaching and the brain: Promoting authentic engagement and rigor among culturally and linguistically diverse students*. Corwin.

Heath, C., & Heath, D. (2010). *Switch: How to change things when change is hard*. Broadway Books.

Hewlett Foundation. (2013, April 23). *Deeper learning competencies* [Strategy paper]. https://hewlett.org/wp-content/uploads/2016/08/Deeper_Learning_Defined__April_2013.pdf

High Tech High Graduate School of Education. (n.d.). *Deeper learning competencies* [Graphic]. Deeper Learning. https://deeper-learning.org/

High Tech High Unboxed. (2019, November 4). Ben Daley has learned some things about school improvement [Podcast episode]. *High Tech High Unboxed*. https://podcasts.apple.com/us/podcast/ben-daley-has-learned-some-things-about-school-improvement/id1479866463?i=1000455917425

hooks, b. (1994). *Teaching to transgress: Education as the practice of freedom*. Routledge.

HQPBL. (n.d.). *A framework for high quality project based learning*. https://hqpbl.org/wp-content/uploads/2018/03/FrameworkforHQPBL.pdf

Hsu, L., & McNamara, T. (2016). Starting a school year of deeper learning for teachers. In J. A. Bellanca (Ed.), *Connecting the dots: Teacher effectiveness and deeper professional learning*. Solution Tree Press.

Huberman, M., Bitter, C., Anthony, J., & O'Day, J. (2014). *The shape of deeper learning: Strategies, structures, and cultures in deeper learning network high schools* (Report 1). American Institutes for Research. https://www.air.org/sites/default/files/downloads/report/Report%201%20The%20Shape%20of%20Deeper%20Learning_9-23-14v2.pdf

Ivy Street School. (n.d.). Mission and vision. https://www.ivystreetschool.org/mission-and-vision/

Kamps, K. (2021, January 27). *Promoting a PBL mindset: The "dimmer switch" approach*. PBLWorks. https://www.pblworks.org/blog/promoting-pbl-mindset-dimmer-switch-approach

Killion, J. S. (2018). *Assessing impact: Evaluating professional learning*. Corwin.

Kingston, S. (2018). Project based learning & student achievement: What does the research tell us? *PBL Evidence Matters, 1*(1), 1–11. http://files.eric.ed.gov/fulltext/ED590832.pdf

Kingston, S., & Wagner, K. (2021). *District PBL evidence framework toolkit*. Buck Institute for Education. https://www.pblworks.org/research-district-pbl-evidence-framework-toolkit

KQED. (1999). Making the grade (Episode 112). In KQED, *Bay Window*.

Larmer, J. (2019, April 26). *The elephant in the room: Grading in project based learning*. PBLWorks. https://www.pblworks.org/blog/elephant-room-grading-project-based-learning

Larmer, J., Mergendoller, J. R., & Boss, S. (2015). *Setting the standard for project based learning: A proven approach to rigorous classroom instruction*. ASCD; Buck Institute for Education.

Learning Policy Institute. (n.d.). *Deeper learning*. https://learningpolicyinstitute.org/topic/deeper-learning

Lenz, B. (2014a, March 21). *How assessment can lead to deeper learning*. Edutopia. https://www.edutopia.org/blog/how-assessment-can-lead-to-deeper-learning-bob-lenz

Lenz, B. (2014b, May 20). *The power of performance assessments*. Edutopia. https://www.edutopia.org/blog/the-power-of-performance-assessments-bob-lenz

Levin, S., Leung, M., Edgerton, A. K., & Scott, C. (2020). *Elementary school principals' professional learning: Current status and future needs*. Learning Policy Institute & National Association of Elementary School Principals. https://learningpolicyinstitute.org/sites/default/files/product-files/NAESP_Elementary_Principals_Professional_Learning_REPORT.pdf

Lucas Education Research. (2021). *Project-based learning boosts student achievement in AP courses* [Research brief]. https://www.lucasedresearch.org/docs/kia_brief/

Netolicky, D. M. (2022, March 23). *Key concepts for leading professional learning*. The édu flâneuse. https://theeduflaneuse.com/2022/03/23/key-concepts-for-leading-professional-learning

PBLWorks. (n.d.). *Our racial equity imperative*. https://www.pblworks.org/our-racial-equity-imperative

Petrokubi, J., Denton, A., Holmgren, M., & Taylor, S. (2020). *Scaling high-quality project based learning for deeper learning impact*. PBLWorks. https://www.pblworks.org/sites/default/files/2021-07/Scaling_HQPBL_Final%20Report_12.18.20.pdf

Richardson, W., Bathon, J., & McLeod, S. (2021). *Leadership for deeper learning*. Routledge.

Rogers, E. M. (2003). *Diffusion of innovations* (5th ed.). The Free Press.

Saavedra, A. R., Liu, Y., Haderlein, S. H., Rapaport, A., Garland, M., Hoepfner, D., Morgan, K. L., & Hu, A. (2021). *Knowledge in Action efficacy study over two years*. USC Dornsife Center for Economic and Social Research. https://cesr.usc.edu/sites/default/files/Knowledge%20in%20Action%20Efficacy%20Study_18feb2021_final.pdf

Safir, S. (2017). *The listening leader: Creating the conditions for equitable school transformation*. Jossey-Bass.

Safir, S. (2019, March 6). Street data: A new grammar for educational equity. *EdWeek*. https://www.edweek.org/leadership/opinion-street-data-a-new-grammar-for-educational-equity/2019/03

Safir, S., & Dugan, J. (2021). *Street data: A next-generation model for equity, pedagogy, and school transformation*. Corwin.

Sedita, J. (2020, June 12). *Literacy and equity in education*. Keys to Literacy. https://keystoliteracy.com/blog/literacy-and-equity-in-education/

Senge, P. (1990). *The fifth discipline: The art and practice of the learning organization*. Doubleday/Currency.

Senge, P. M. (2006). *The fifth discipline: The art and practice of the learning organization*. Doubleday/Currency.

Sliwka, A., Klopsch, B., Beigel, J., & Tung, L. (2024, January). Transformational leadership for deeper learning: Shaping innovative school practices for enhanced learning. *Journal of Educational Administration, 62*(1), 103–121. https://doi.org/10.1108/JEA-03-2023-0049

Thomas, J. W. (2000). *A review of research on project based learning*. PBLWorks. https://my.pblworks.org/resource/document/a_review_of_research_on_project_based_learning

Wagner, K., & Kingston, S. (2023). *School PBL evidence framework toolkit*. Buck Institute for Education. https://www.pblworks.org/school-pbl-evidence-framework-toolkit

Willis, L., Badrinarayan, A., & Martinez, M. (2022). *Quality criteria for systems of performance assessment for school, district, and network leaders*. Learning Policy Institute. https://learningpolicyinstitute.org/product/quality-criteria-performance-assessment-systems-tool

Wolfson, A. R., & Carskadon, M. A. (1998). Sleep schedules and daytime functioning in adolescents. *Child Development, 69*(4), 875–887. https://doi.org/10.1111/j.1467-8624.1998.tb06149.x

Women@Forbes Files. (2014, December 19). *Why data matters*. Forbes. https://www.forbes.com/sites/forbeswomanfiles/2014/12/19/why-data-matters

Yang, R., Zeiser, K. L., & Siman, N. (2016). *Deeper learning and college enrollment: What happens after high school?* American Institutes for Research. https://www.air.org/sites/default/files/downloads/report/Deeper-Learning-Postsecondary-Appendix-August-2016-rev.pdf

Yoon, K. S., Duncan, T., Lee, S. W.-Y., Scarloss, B., & Shapley, K. L. (2007, October). *Reviewing the evidence on how teacher professional development affects student achievement* (Issues & Answers Report REL 2007–No. 033). Institute of Education Sciences. https://web.archive.org/web/20250202035724/https://ies.ed.gov/ncee/edlabs/regions/southwest/pdf/rel_2007033.pdf

Zeiser, K. L., Mills, N., Wulach, S., & Garet, M. S. (2016). *Graduation advantage persists for students in deeper learning network high schools: Updated findings from the Study of Deeper Learning: Opportunities and Outcomes*. American Institutes for Research. https://www.air.org/sites/default/files/downloads/report/Graduation-Advantage-Persists-Deeper-Learning-Report-March-2016-rev.pdf

Zeiser, K. L., Taylor, J., Rickles, J., Garet, M. S., & Segeritz, M. (2014). *Evidence of deeper learning outcomes* (Report 3). American Institutes for Research. https://www.air.org/sites/default/files/downloads/report/Report_3_Evidence_of_Deeper_Learning_Outcomes.pdf

Index

The letter *f* following a page locator denotes a figure.

academic success skills criteria
    data collection, analysis, and use, 123, 124*f*, 125
    PBL Evidence Framework, 121, 122*f*
adopter category chart, 201–202
adult learning structures, 71–74, 71*f*, 72*f*
agency, 47, 49
assessment
    elements of, 107*f*
    equity and access in, 106–107
    exemplars in, 106
    grading for, 110–112
    implementation, 147–149, 185–188
    leadership practices for, 107*f*
    performance, 108–110, 112–115, 140
    pillars of, 106–108
    rubrics in, 106

behaviors, mental models and, 20

capacity, building
    assessing deeper learning and, 102–115
    district leaders and effective, 147–150, 148*f*
    District Logic Model, 15*f*, 141*f*
    Gold Standard PBL, 83–96, 100
    in infrastructure design, 63–64, 66*f*
    meaning of, 83
    in others, 21–22
change, holonomy and symmetry in, 12–13
classroom, shared power in the, 8*f*, 10
classroom walkthrough strategy, 128
coaching and feedback, 91–94
cognitive demand
    Equity Lever of, 8*f*, 9
    reflecting on for implementation, 160–161

collaboration
    element of culture, 50–51
    in teacher planning, 69–70
community of practice approach, 95
continuous improvement
    benefits of, 133
    District PBL Evidence Framework Toolkit, 150–151, 152*f*
    in infrastructure design, 64, 66*f*
    PBLWorks District Logic Model, 15*f*, 141*f*, 150–151, 150*f*, 153–154
continuous improvement, measuring impact for. *See also* vision
    data collection limitations, 118–119
    elements of, 124*f*
    implementation management, 124*f*, 126–128
    leadership practices, 124*f*
    PBL Evidence Framework, using the, 119–121
    in practice, 136
    processes, 128–133, 129*f*, 131*f*, 132*f*
continuous improvement processes
    classroom walkthrough strategy, 128
    implement and collect data phase, 130
    leadership learning walks for, 129
    leadership stories, 133–135
    planning phase, 130
    refinement phase, 130–133, 132*f*
    reflection phase, 130, 131*f*
    short-cycle improvement process, 129–130, 129*f*
culture
    District Logic Model, 15*f*, 141*f*
    elements of, 48*f*
    in infrastructure design, 62–63, 65*f*
    risk-taking and growth in, 49–50

culture, building
    celebrating success, 53–54
    collaboration element, 50–51
    district leaders and effective, 145–147, 146f
    leadership practices, 48f
    making student work visible, 52–56
    in practice, 57–58, 57f, 58f
    process of, 46–47
    shared responsibility in, 50–51
    student agency and, 47, 49
    trust in, 49–50

data collection, analysis, and use. *See also* impact, measuring for continuous improvement
    academic and success skills criteria, 123, 124f, 125
    Data Collection Plan sample, 179–181
    for improvement, 118–119
deeper learning
    competencies, 34–36, 35f
    competencies of, 1–2
    meaning of, 1–2
    results of, 2, 26–27, 38
deeper learning, assessing
    building capacity, 102–115
    in practice, 115–116
    practices comprising, 103–104
    purpose of, 102–103
    requirements for, 103
    research findings, 104–105
    student agency in, 106
deeper learning for all, meaning of, 2, 13
diffusion of innovations theory, 143
district leaders, implementation and. *See also* PBLWorks District Logic Model
    capacity building, 147–150, 148f
    continuous improvement, 150–151, 150f, 153–154
    culture, developing the, 145–147, 146f
    vision, developing a, 141–145, 142f
district leadership. *See also* leadership
    Equity Levers for, 8f
    knowledge, reflecting on for implementation, 160
    in practice, 156
    swing, creating, 140–141
    translating leadership practices for coherence, 139–140
District Logic Model, Strategic Leadership Framework, 15–16, 15f

equity
    in assessment, 106
    effectiveness, PBL as a lever for, 5–7, 27
    Racial Equity Imperative, PBLWorks, 6f
    reflecting on for implementation, 159–160

Equity Levers
    cognitive demand, 8f, 9
    knowledge of students, 7, 8f, 9
    literacy, 8f, 9–10
    shared power, 8f, 10
exemplars, in assessment, 106

feedback, 91–94

Gold Standard PBL
    capacity building, 85f, 98–99
    framework, 4f
    leadership stories, 96–98
    project based teaching practices, 88–89, 90f, 91, 174–178
    project design elements, 86, 87f, 88
    project design rubric, 171–173
grading, 110–112. *See also* assessment
graduate profiles, 34f

helpful feedback, 92–93
holonomy, 12–13
HQPBL (high-quality PBL), 3, 5, 13, 14f

Ideal Graduate Profile, 35–36, 35f
impact, measuring for continuous improvement. *See also* vision
    continuous improvement processes, 128–133, 129f
    data collection limitations, 118–119
    elements of, 124f
    implementation management, 124f, 126–128
    leadership practices, 124f
    PBL Evidence Framework, using the, 119–121
    in practice, 136
implement and collect data phase of continuous improvement, 130
implementation
    action planning, 162–164
    adopter categories, 143
    assessments, 147–149, 185–188
    coherent, 147
    expectations in, 9
    formula for success, 120f
    leadership for, 84–85
    leading indicators criteria, 121, 122f, 126–128
    opinion leaders in, 143–144
    progress indicators, 121, 122f
    readiness criteria, 121, 122f
    requirements for, 9, 84
    scaling districtwide, 144
    School Conditions Inventory, 65–66f
implementation management, 124f, 126–128
implementation tools
    adopter category chart, 201–202
    Adoption Curve, determining the, 203–205

implementation tools (*continued*)
    Communication Plan, 206
    District Conditions Inventory, 189–190
    District PBL Readiness Checklist, 191–192
    Implementation Pulse Survey, 127, 182–184
    opinion leaders, identifying, 202
    PBL Action Plan Template, 163, 198–200
    PBL School Implementation Planning Tool, 163, 193–197
infrastructure, critical levers for
    adult learning structures, 70–71, 71*f*
    collaborative teacher planning, 69–70
    the master schedule, 67, 68*f*, 69
    professional learning and development, 70–74, 72*f*
    resource allocation, 74–76
infrastructure, designing the
    building in practice, 80–81
    capacity building, 63–64, 66*f*
    continuous improvement, 64, 66*f*
    culture in, 62–63, 65*f*
    for implementation, 61–62
    vision in, 62, 65*f*
innovation, characteristics of, 203–205
instructional system, coherent, 139–140
Ivy Street School, 41–43

KDR (Know-Do-Reflect) framework, 105, 108
kind feedback, 92
knowledge of students
    Equity Lever of, 7, 8*f*, 9
    reflecting on for implementation, 160

leadership. *See also* district leadership; school leaders
    advocacy for students, 38–39, 41–43
    commitment to PBL in, 39–41
    focus, creative tension in, 23–25, 24*f*
    mindsets and, 19–21, 28, 83–84
    professional development, investing in, 22
    risk-taking, trust, and growth, encouraging, 49–50
    targeting simultaneous, correlated outcomes, 25–27, 26*f*
leadership capacity, building
    to build capacity in others, 21–22
    rubric design, 112
    for teacher performance assessment, 109–110, 112
leadership development, 94–96
leadership learning walks, 128–129
leadership stories
    advocacy for students, 41–43
    continuous improvement processes, 133–135
    Gold Standard PBL, 96–98
    increasing rigor and relevance through PBL, 154–155
    making student work visible, 54–56
    performance assessment, 112–115
    rethinking time, 76–77, 78*f*, 79–80
    rubrics, 112–115
Leadership Theory of Action, PBL Works, 11–12, 12*f*
leading indicators criteria, PBL Evidence Framework, 121, 122*f*, 126–128
learning partnerships, building with students, 9
literacy
    Equity Lever of, 8*f*, 9–10
    reflecting on for implementation, 161

the master schedule, 67, 68*f*, 69
mental models, working with, 19–21
mindsets
    leadership and, 19–21, 28, 83–84
    mental models and, 19–21
    reframing in practice, 28
motivation, intrinsic, 106

North Star, 32, 41, 62, 141. *See also* vision

opinion leaders in implementation, 143–144, 202

PBL Adoption Curve, determining, 203–205
PBL Communication Plan, 206
PBL Evidence Framework
    components, 121, 122*f*, 123
    key assumption, 120–121
    website, 119
PBL Implementation Pulse Survey, 127, 182–184
PBLWorks District Logic Model
    capacity building, 147–150, 148*f*
    components, 141*f*
    continuous improvement, 150–151, 150*f*, 153–154
    culture, developing the, 145–147, 146*f*
    introduction, 140–141
    vision, developing a, 141–145, 142*f*
PBLWorks District PBL Evidence Framework Toolkit, 150–151, 152*f*
PBLWorks Policy and Initiative Self-Assessment, 185–188
PBLWorks Project Design Rubric, 171–173
performance assessment, 108–110, 112–115, 140
physical spaces, rethinking, 75
planning phase of continuous improvement, 130

Polynesian Voyaging Society, 31–32
power, shared
    in the classroom, 8*f*, 10
    Equity Lever of, 8*f*, 10
    with leaders and teachers, 8*f*, 10
    reflecting on for implementation, 161–162
professional development, 22, 72–74, 88–89
professional learning
    coaching and feedback, 91–94
    in house, preparing for, 92
    leadership cadre development, 94–96, 99
Professional Learning Loop, 71, 72*f*
Project Based Learning (PBL)
    key to success, xii–xiii
    leadership commitment to, 39–41
    relentless, 17–18
    results of, xi–xii, 3, 104–105
    sustainability, requirements for, 14
    vignettes, xi–xii
    vision statement, 32

Racial Equity Imperative, PBL Works, 6*f*
readiness criteria, PBL Evidence Framework, 121, 122*f*
refinement phase of continuous improvement, 130–132, 132*f*
reflection, relentless, 17–18, 159–162
reflection phase of continuous improvement, 130, 131*f*
resource allocation, 74–76
responsibility, sharing, 50–51
risk-taking and growth, 49–50
rubrics
    in assessment, 111–112
    leadership stories, 112–115

School Conditions Inventory, 65–66*f*
school leaders. *See also* leadership
    effective, research on, 11
    Equity Levers for, 8*f*
    Leadership Theory of Action, 11–12, 12*f*
    sharing power with, 8*f*, 10
    Strategic Leadership Framework, 13–14, 14*f*
    transformational, as accelerators of change, 10–11
specific feedback, 92
standardized testing, 25–27, 26*f*, 120

Strategic Leadership Framework, PBL Works
    District Logic Model, 15–16, 15*f*
    nested approach, 13–14, 14*f*
student agency, 47, 49, 106
student knowledge
    Equity Lever of, 7, 8*f*, 9
    reflecting on for implementation, 160
students
    advocacy for, 38–39, 41–43
    future-ready, requirements for, 2
    learning partnerships, building with students, 9
student work, making visible, 52–56
success, celebrating, 53–54
success skills criteria
    data collection, analysis, and use, 123, 124*f*, 125
    PBL Evidence Framework, 121, 122*f*
swing, creating, 140–141
symmetry, 12–13

teachers
    agency, 47
    coaching and support, 75–76, 91–94
    Equity Levers for, 8*f*
    knowledge, reflecting on for implementation, 160
    learning about, 92
    resource allocation for, 75–76
    sharing power with, 8*f*, 10
teaching practices, project based
    Gold Standard PBL, 88–89, 90*f*, 91
    rubric, 174–178
time, rethinking
    collaborative teacher planning, 69–70
    leadership stories, 76–77, 78*f*, 79–80
    the master schedule, 67, 68*f*, 69
training, leaders participation in, 88–89
trust, 49–50

vision. *See also* leadership
    crafting the, 30–32, 33*f*, 43
    creative tension in, 23–24, 24*f*
    developing for student outcomes, 35–36, 35*f*
    District Logic Model, 15*f*, 141–145, 141*f*
    in infrastructure design, 62, 65*f*
    personal and shard, 36–38

walkthrough strategies, 128–129

About the Authors

Bob Lenz is the CEO of PBLWorks (formerly Buck Institute for Education), the leader in preparing teachers, schools, and districts to implement high-quality project based learning in K–12 education. Recognized as an expert in project based learning and school redesign, Bob co-authored *Transforming Schools Using Project-Based Learning, Performance Assessment, and Common Core Standards.*

Bob's commitment to advancing racial equity in education has driven his efforts to expand deeper learning for all students. He travels throughout the country and internationally to speak about the power of project based learning to transform learning and lives.

Bob's early career as a middle and high school teacher inspired him to co-found Envision Education, which developed innovative project based schools in the San Francisco Bay Area. Envision empowers students to become the first in their family to attend and graduate from college. Bob served as Envision's CEO and chief of innovation from 2001 to 2015.

The importance of Bob's work has been recognized and furthered through projects funded by the Hewlett Foundation, Stuart Foundation, Gates Foundation, W. K. Kellogg Foundation, James Irvine Foundation, Carnegie Foundation for the Advancement of Teaching, Project Management Institute Educational Foundation, ECMC Foundation, and Harold K. L. Castle Foundation.

Bob grew up on the island of Catalina, off the coast of Southern California, and now lives near San Francisco. Now that their children are grown, he and his wife have more time for raising their breeder guide dog, following rugby matches across the world, cycling, and stand-up paddleboarding.

Dr. Lisa Mireles is the senior director of professional learning design and senior advisor to the CEO at PBLWorks. She is recognized as an expert in leadership for project based learning and in leveraging digital tools to accelerate deeper learning. A seasoned school and district leader, Lisa co-founded the Kauaʻi Educational Leadership Alliance and the Hawaiʻi chapter of the Society for Technology in Education. She has also helped lead Hawaiʻi's Schools of the Future conference for over a decade.

Lisa's early career as a bilingual high school teacher in Oxnard, California, solidified her belief in the power of constructivist, student-centered learning. She refined her practice while teaching internationally at Surabaya Intercultural School in Surabaya, Indonesia, and the American School of Bombay in Mumbai, India, where she helped establish International Baccalaureate programs and a 1:1 laptop initiative.

In Hawaiʻi, she guided a small, independent school to become a model School of the Future that integrated project based learning and supported the leaders at Kapaʻa High School in implementing an academy model. She worked with Hawaiian-focused charter schools as a school improvement specialist for Kamehameha Schools and as a school renewal specialist for the Hawaiʻi Department of Education, supporting schools on Kauaʻi.

Lisa grew up in Southern California and now lives on the island of Kauaʻi. She enjoys spending time at the beach, line dancing, reading, and hanging out with her grown children, who returned to the islands after college.

About PBLWorks

The Buck Institute for Education/PBLWorks believes that all students, especially Black and Brown students, should have access to high-quality project based learning to deepen their learning and achieve success in college, career, and life. Its focus is on building the capacity of teachers to design and facilitate high-quality project based learning, and on supporting school and system leaders in creating the conditions for all students to succeed.

Related Resources

At the time of publication, the following resources were available (ASCD stock numbers in parentheses):

Design Thinking for School Leaders: Five Roles and Mindsets That Ignite Positive Change by Alyssa Gallagher and Kami Thordarson (#118022)

Designed to Learn: Using Design Thinking to Bring Purpose and Passion to the Classroom by Lindsay Portnoy (#120026)

Designing Authentic Performance Tasks and Projects: Tools for Meaningful Learning and Assessment by Jay McTighe, Kristina J. Doubet, and Eric M. Carbaugh (#119021)

Everyday Problem-Based Learning: Quick Projects to Build Problem-Solving Fluency by Brian Pete and Robin Fogarty (#117057)

Getting Started with Project Based Learning (Quick Reference Guide) by John Larmer (#QRG117106)

Learning They'll Love: Engage Students, Meet Standards, and Spark Creativity with Personal Interest Projects by Elizabeth Agro Radday (#125019)

Project Based Teaching: How to Create Rigorous and Engaging Learning Experiences by Suzie Boss with John Larmer (#118047)

Real-World Projects: How do I design relevant and engaging learning experiences (ASCD Arias) by Suzie Boss (#SF115043E4)

The Relevant Classroom: 6 Steps to Foster Real-World Learning by Eric Hardie (#120003)

Setting the Standard for Project Based Learning: A Proven Approach to Rigorous Classroom Instruction by John Larmer, John Mergendoller, and Suzie Boss (#114017)

For up-to-date information about ASCD resources, go to www.ascd.org. You can search the complete archives of *Educational Leadership* at www.ascd.org/el. To contact us, send an email to member@ascd.org or call 1-800-933-2723 or 703-578-9600.

DON'T MISS A SINGLE ISSUE OF THIS AWARD-WINNING MAGAZINE.

iste+ascd
educational leadership

If you belong to a Professional Learning Community, you may be looking for a way to get your fellow educators' minds around a complex topic. Why not delve into a relevant theme issue of *Educational Leadership*, the journal written by educators for educators?

Subscribe now and browse or purchase back issues of our flagship publication at **www.ascd.org/el**. Discounts on bulk purchases are available.

iste+ascd

Arlington, VA USA
1-800-933-2723

www.ascd.org
www.iste.org